THE B2B Social Media Book →

Become a Marketing Superstar

by Generating Leads with
Blogging, LinkedIn,
Twitter, Facebook,
E-Mail, and More

Kipp Bodnar and Jeffrey L. Cohen

WILEY

John Wiley & Sons, Inc.

Published by John Wiley & Sons, Inc., Hoboken, New Jersey.
Published simultaneously in Canada.

For general information on our other products and services or for technical support, please contact our Customer Care Department within the United States at (800) 762–2974, outside the United States at (317) 572–3993 or fax (317) 572–4002.

Wiley publishes in a variety of print and electronic formats and by print-on-demand. Some material included with standard print versions of this book may not be included in ebooks or in print-on-demand. If this book refers to media such as a CD or DVD that is not included in the version you purchased, you may download this material at http://booksupport.wiley.com. For more information about Wiley products, visit www.wiley.com.

Library of Congress Cataloging-in-Publication Data:

Bodnar, Kipp, 1982-
     The B2B social media book : become a marketing superstar by generating leads with blogging, Linkedin, Twitter, Facebook, e-mail, and more / Kipp Bodnar and Jeffrey L. Cohen.
         p.   cm.
     ISBN 978–1–118–16776–2 (cloth); ISBN 978–1–118–21378–0 (ebk);
     ISBN 978–1–118–21393–3 (ebk); ISBN 978–1–118–21430–5 (ebk)
         1. Internet marketing.   2. Social media—Economic aspects.   3. Online social networks—Economic aspects.   I. Cohen, Jeffrey L., 1965-   II. Title.
     HF5415.1265.B633   2012
     658.8'72—dc23

                                                                    2011037191

Printed in the United States of America

10   9   8   7   6   5   4   3   2   1

For my parents who taught me how to learn and teach.
And for Tera, who constantly makes me better at both.

—K.B.

For Peter and Grace, even though you are not B2B
marketers, you wound up in my book.

—J.L.C.

Contents

Foreword   ANN HANDLEY   **xi**

Introduction   **We Didn't Wake Up One Day**   **xv**
              and Write This Book

How We Got Here   *xvi*
This Book Is an Offer   *xvii*
You Want More Examples?   *xvii*
What Did We Miss?   *xviii*
Are You Ready to Go?   *xviii*

I The Fundamentals of Social Media Lead Generation   **1**

1 Why B2B Is Better at Social Media Than B2C   **3**

The Marketing Status Quo   *3*
What Your Marketing Could Be   *4*
Five Reasons B2B Companies Are a Better Fit for Social   *4*
    Media Marketing Than B2C Companies
When Social Media Isn't Right for B2B   *6*
B2B Social Media as an Annuity   *8*
Results Independent of Effort   *8*
Annuities Facilitate Scale   *9*
Social Media Is Only One Piece   *9*
Building a Next-Generation B2B Marketing Team   *10*
Storytelling + Data Analysis = Great Social Media Marketer   *10*
The Perfect B2B Marketing Leader   *11*
Three B2B Social Media Steps to Superstardom   *11*

2 Five-Step Social Media Lead Generation Process   **13**

Step 1: Getting the Basics Right   *14*
Step 2: Maximize Content Discovery   *17*
Step 3: Create Conversion Ubiquity   *21*

Step 4: Test and Fail Fast 22
Step 5: Optimize for Maximum Lead Flow 25
Three B2B Social Media Lead Generation Steps to Superstardom 27

3 Yes, Chapter 3 in a Social Media Book Is about 29
Search (It's That Important!)

Evolution of Search 29
Context as the Foundation of Search 29
Four On-Page Optimization Opportunities 30
Authority Drives Ranking 32
Three Strategies for Link Building Success 33
Changing Authority 34
Social Search and B2B 35
Unified Keyword Strategy 35
Rank Is Dead 37
Search Isn't Just Google 38
Three B2B Search Engine Optimization Steps to Superstardom 39

4 How to Close the Loop of Social Media ROI 41

The Math of ROI 42
Calculating COCA 42
Understanding Total Lifetime Value 43
Social Media Is Good for COCA and TLV 46
Intent Is Attribution 47
First- versus Last-Action Attribution 48
Gathering the Data 49
Measuring to Superstardom 50
Integrating Marketing and Sales Databases 50
It Is Math, Not Hugs 51
Three B2B Social Media ROI Steps to Superstardom 52

5 Reach: More Is Always Better 55

Being Targeted Isn't Enough 55
Be Able to Sell Anything 56
Six Time-Tested Methods for Building Reach 57
Remarkable and Frequent Content Fuels Reach 58
Paying for Reach Is Okay 59
Nearsightedness Kills Great Marketing 61
Three B2B Social Media Reach Building Steps to Superstardom 61

II Social Media Lead Generation in Action 63

6 Creating Ebooks and Webinars That Prospects Love 65

Create Ebooks Everyone Wants 66
The 10-Step Blueprint to Ebook Awesomeness 67

Webinars Are Low-Cost Trade Shows 69
Five Steps for an Engaging Webinar 70
Marketing with Existing Sales Tools 71
Storytelling with Video 71
Three Commandments of B2B Video 72
To YouTube or Not to YouTube, That Is the Question 73
Being Interesting Is the New Black 74
Three B2B Social Media Content Offer Steps to Superstardom 74

7 **Why You Are Already a Business Blogging Expert 77**
The Origins of Corporate Blogging 78
The Thinking Part of Setting Up Your Business Blog 79
The Content Part of Setting Up Your Blog 80
The Nuts and Bolts Part of Setting Up Your Blog 82
The Ultimate Business Blogging Checklist 84
Blog Content Drives Leads 95
Three B2B Blogging Steps to Superstardom 96

8 **Become a LinkedIn Lead Generation Superstar 97**
Profiles Are Just the Beginning 97
Companies Can Get Recommendations Too 100
Business Value Through Sharing 102
Grouping Your Expertise: LinkedIn Groups 103
Answering the Questions: LinkedIn Answers 105
Professionals Need Advertising Too 106
Three B2B LinkedIn Steps to Superstardom 108

9 **Twitter: Leads in 140 Characters 109**
Five Off-Platform Benefits of Twitter 110
Anatomy of a Tweet 111
Replies and Mentions 112
Retweets 113
Direct Messages 114
Hashtags 114
Finding B2B Leads on Twitter 115
Setting Up a B2B Twitter Account 116
The 10-4-1 Rule of Social Sharing 117
14 Ways to Drive Leads with Content on Twitter 118
Five Ideas for Prospect Engagement for B2B Companies 123
Pushing the Twitter Envelope 124
Three B2B Twitter Steps to Superstardom 126

10 **Maximizing Facebook Lead Generation through Engagement 127**
Profiles versus Pages 127

It Made Sense for Cisco to Join   128
Three Reasons to Create a B2B Presence on Facebook   128
Yes, Facebook Is for B2B   129
Understanding the EdgeRank Engagement Algorithm   130
10 Ways to Drive Leads on Facebook   131
Facebook Engagement Means Leads   138
Three B2B Social Media Facebook Steps to Superstardom   141

11 E-Mail Is Social   **143**
Opt-In Is a Better Call to Action   143
Why Nobody Likes E-Mail   145
12 Ways to Get More Leads Out of E-Mail   145
Testing E-Mail Ideas Using Social Media   148
Four Ways to Socialize a Prospect's Inbox   149
Social Profiles within the Inbox   150
Three B2B Social Media E-Mail Steps to Superstardom   151

**III Taking Social Media Lead Generation   153
to the Next Level**

12 Stop Preparing for the Mobile Web; It's Here   **155**
Getting Smart about Smartphones   155
Two Ways to Mobile-Optimize a Website   157
On the Go with Mobile Content   159
What Is the Context of Your Content?   161
Rethinking the Mobile Landing Page   161
B2B Mobile Apps Are for Suckers   163
Location Is for Sales, Not Marketing   164
Three B2B Social Media Mobile Marketing Steps to Superstardom   165

13 Making Trade Shows Social   **167**
Driving Trade Show Leads with Social Media   167
Treat Trade Shows Like Comarketing   168
Five Steps to Instantly Make Your Trade Show More Social   169
Taking Over Physical and Digital Word of Mouth   170
Three Trade Show Takeaways from "DNS Is Sexy"   172
Using Location to Become the Best "Party" at a Trade Show   172
Virtual Conference   173
Three B2B Social Media Trade Show Steps to Superstardom   175

14 Run a B2B Social Media Marketing Team Like   **177**
a Start-Up
It All Starts with Passion   177
Where Does Passion Come From?   179

Knowing When to Ship 180
It Becomes Agile Marketing Anyway 181
Three Principles of Agile Marketing 181
When It's Time to Look for Funding 182
What's the Exit Strategy? 183
Three B2B Social Media Start-Up Steps to Superstardom 184

15 10 B2B Social Media Roadblocks **185**
1. Legal Wants Full Approval—Of Everything 185
2. Social Network Access Is Blocked 186
3. Executive Support Is Lacking 187
4. The Customer Base Is Not Attuned to Social Media 187
5. But I Have a Real Job to Do 188
6. It Is Free, Right? 188
7. We Need the Right People for the Task 189
8. We Have Always Done It This Way 190
9. The Network Admin Is a Debbie Downer 190
10. You Don't Know Where to Start 191
Three Clearing Roadblock Steps to Superstardom 193

16 The Best Time Ever! **195**
Social Media Marketing Is about Lead Generation 196
Be a Storyteller Who Uses Data 196
Second Is the First Loser 197
Useless Metrics 197
The Beginning, Not the End 198

Acknowledgments **201**

About the Authors **203**

Notes **205**

Index **209**

Foreword

This is the book I've been waiting for.

Does that sound like a bloated overstatement? It's not. It's true.

Ever since social media tools started to emerge in the business world, they've been simultaneously pilloried and championed, scorned and lionized—depending on your point of view or the kind of business you're in.

And that's part of the problem, isn't it?

Social tools and platforms have helped sell airline seats on Southwest, shoes on Zappos, T-shirts on Threadless, or laptops on Dell.com. But those high-profile consumer-based success stories are easily dismissed by business-to-business (B2B) types who don't see the same link between social media and B2B sales.

How can a set of tools that puts butts in airline seats actually make a difference in the B2B world? How can a platform that racks up T-shirt sales matter to me? What works so well for one can't possibly work for the other, right?

Wrong. This is why I started this foreword saying that this is a book I've been anticipating. (And I'm thrilled that it's here and that you're now reading it, of course.)

The truth is that social media can be as perfectly aligned to B2B sales as a ball bearing is to its groove. And here's why.

B2B businesses don't facilitate one-off deals like T-shirts or flip-flops. Rather, they build relationships for pricier, more complex, and longer-term sales. They educate their prospects and act as a resource to them throughout the decision process. In short, they lay the groundwork for a long-term relationship, not a one-off transaction.

In that way, as a B2B marketer you are way ahead of the curve—or at least your business-to-consumer (B2C) brethren. You are already in the business of generating leads and nurturing them. You already have a crystal clear understanding of who your customer is. You already have the kind of in-house expertise you need to create content that will resonate with your prospects because it's what they crave. You already have a perspective and point of view that differentiates your brand.

Social media, then, is an opportunity—not a burden. Social media gives you a new way to reach more people, to hone what you already know and share it with your audience in a new way, to amplify what you already are saying, to engage and be enjoyably interesting, to be human, to have a little fun—and so to connect with your prospects and customers in a powerful way.

I didn't use the phrase *enjoyably interesting* lightly in that last sentence. Creating fun and interesting content and amplifying its reach with social tools can humanize your business. It can give you an opportunity to show personality and point of view in an appealing, engaging way that sets you apart from your competitors. Since your content is often on the front lines—it's what reaches your prospects even before your sales team— "enjoyably interesting" can be a differentiator in the B2B space. (See the stories in this book for more specifics on what I'm talking about.)

I didn't use the word *powerful* in that previous paragraph lightly either. Because I believe that social media does indeed have the power to transform your B2B company in significant ways. The problem is that many companies get caught up in the tools: How can we possibly sell solder paste on Twitter? What's the use of a Facebook group for our enterprise software solution? But the tools are merely that: tools. The real benefit— as with any other gizmo—comes from how you use it.

And that's where this book comes in. This is the book that strips out the hype surrounding tools and platforms and shows you—with how-to blueprints and frameworks—how you can generate and nurture business leads through social media. It shows you how you can integrate social media with your existing programs. It shows you how you can use content you create to educate and nurture prospects. And—*bonus!*—it spells out how you, the B2B marketer, can be the hero at your company because the marketing department will be contributing to the bottom line in a tangible, measurable way.

As someone who has spent most of her career as a writer and editor for B2B publications, I'm practically allergic to content that doesn't deliver on the how-to. I'm talking about books or articles or any kind of content that's all strategy and theory and never quite manages to offer a blueprint or implementation framework.

Theory has its place, of course. But in my experience, businesses are more anxious to know *how* to do something (*how* to build a client base, *how* to create momentum, *how* to grow revenue) than they are interested in knowledge for the sake of pure intellectual curiosity.

Kipp Bodnar and Jeff Cohen are doers, and they deliver on their promise to show you *how*, not just *why*. I love that.

You're going to love it, too. But more important, you're going to *use* it. It's going to matter. It's going to make a difference. So . . . get to it!

—**Ann Handley**
Chief Content Officer, MarketingProfs;
Coauthor of *Content Rules:
How to Create Killer Blogs, Podcasts, Videos, Ebooks,
Webinars (and More) That Engage Customers and Ignite
Your Business* (John Wiley & Sons, Inc., 2011);

Monthly Lead Gen columnist, *Entrepreneur Magazine*

Introduction

We Didn't Wake Up One Day and Write This Book

Welcome business-to-business (B2B) marketers!

The book you are reading didn't happen overnight. We are so excited we can barely hold back the whoops and the high fives.

In a moment we will tell you how we got here, but to start we wanted to address two things.

First, for those of you who are considering buying this book, if you are happy with the status quo at work, don't want to get noticed, and are not interested in adding to the bottom line of your B2B company, this book isn't for you. We would rather you not buy this book than get frustrated with the possibilities of a future that you are unwilling to invest in. For the rest of you, again, welcome to the most important book you will read this year.

The second thing is to answer the question, Why? Why in the digital millennium, when everything is online, would two online guys write and distribute a traditional book about an online topic?

Even with all the changes that the social web has brought to marketers, from tools to opportunities, there is something comforting about a book. It can sit on your shelf. It can sit on your desk. You can read it at home or on a plane. You can easily share it with a colleague. You can share it with your boss. You can give a copy to your partners, vendors, and customers.

In the current work environment, traditional business books still make sense. The numbers from our publisher bear this out, but of course it is available in an electronic form as well.

How We Got Here

The story of this book starts in the fall of 2008. That's more than three years ago. Think about that in the context of your social media planning. What was your B2B company doing with social media back then? Unless you work for a technology company or a marketing agency, it is unlikely that social media marketing was on your radar.

And what were we doing? After several years of being active in social media on a personal level, both of us were working for B2B marketing agencies, starting to explore how they could use blogging for business. We both knew that most B2B companies had not adopted social media strategies but that it would be coming. Kipp registered the domain SocialMediaB2B.com. Jeff was monitoring Twitter for mentions of B2B. There were only a handful every day.

Early in 2009 we discussed the possibility of starting a blog at Kipp's domain. We were both marketers with a great understanding of social media. We knew that one way to influence adoption by B2B marketers was to share best practices, examples, and new ideas and platforms that could be leveraged for success. We also talked about how the blog could lead to speaking engagements at conferences. And one day could lead us to write a book. The book that we once dreamed of is the one you are holding right now.

We launched the site about a month later to little fanfare. Early posts were thoughtful but uneven as we tried to find both our voice and our audience. Some companies that were profiled at that time are included in this book (Boeing and Indium, to name two). So when we advise marketers that you need to start writing and power through the idea that nobody but your mom is reading, we did it too. Of course, our blog was about B2B marketing, so even our moms didn't read it.

The more we wrote, the more we developed an audience. We started getting traffic from search. Our domain name was the topic of the site. We also made sure that post titles featured keywords. The audience continued to grow, and our voice as experts on social media for B2B companies began to spread. In the spring of 2011 we decided it was time to write this book.

Adoption of social media by B2B companies did not happen as fast as we had expected. Many companies that had started using social media didn't understand why. They didn't understand how to determine the return on investment (ROI). That's because they weren't focused on lead generation. If you are not driving revenue, or leads as their proxy, it is difficult to measure the return. That's why lead generation is the cornerstone of this book.

If you don't want to increase revenue, this book is not for you.

There are many things that social media can do to help a company, and there are many functions that can be enhanced by a social media approach. The problem is that management might not pay for it. Or they might not be able to afford it. If you can start by showing that social media can generate revenue, now you are onto something. Executives understand dollars.

This Book Is an Offer

The biggest difference between our blog and the lessons you will learn as you read this book is that we were focused on education on the blog, not our own lead generation. Our blog posts did not include offers and calls-to-action for almost three years. But guess what? If you bought this book through our site, you might have clicked on one of those calls-to-action. This book is now our offer, and you chose to accept it in exchange for your hard-earned dollars—and now your attention.

We spent three years giving away remarkable content and building an audience for that content. So when we released this book, its purchase became an easy exchange to pay us back for sharing our thoughts and knowledge about social media. The cost of this book is a small price to pay for up to three years of hundreds and hundreds of blog posts that have helped you understand social media in a B2B context.

This book is actionable, including exercises to complete along the way. Because of this, we hope that you will keep this book on your desk, not your bookshelf. We don't want to be only top of mind, but top of desk. This will make it easier to make sure you are completing the steps to marketing superstardom.

You Want More Examples?

Many social media books are filled with interviews and examples of social media success. A good portion of this book establishes the framework and the fundamentals for using social media for lead generation. The examples and interviews we included represent those B2B companies and marketers who understand not just what they are doing but why they are doing it.

The adoption curve for social media for B2B companies has been a lot longer than we anticipated three years ago. On top of that, few companies are successfully using social media for lead generation. If you can master the ideas in this book, marketing superstardom is in your sights.

What Did We Miss?

Just over a month before we finalized this manuscript, Google launched their social network, Google+. It roared out of the gate with huge adoption and many wondered if it was a Facebook killer or a Twitter killer. Incorporating elements of both, plus a requirement to organize your connections from the start in a series of circles, many people enjoyed the experience of building personal profiles and sharing content with their new networks. Part of its early success was due to users' familiarity with social networks. Others wondered where they would find the time for another social network.

Businesses were asked not to set up personal profiles, as robust business profiles were coming soon. As you are reading this, you probably know about business profiles, if Google stuck to their announced timeline. One of the compelling elements of publishing information on Google+ is that you can segment your information by using circles to divide prospects, leads, and customers. The principles of driving business through social media do not change with every new social network that opens.

Are You Ready to Go?

Get ready to learn how social media can change your business and make you a marketing superstar. This book focuses on social media for lead generation. We provide theory, strategy, and tactics, as well as actionable steps to get you started.

These are not small steps. They may be the biggest ones you will take in your career. They will change your perception of marketing. They will change others' perception of you. Self-actualization and career advancement will be achieved through social media lead generation. Those are pretty huge goals for a book. We did our part. Now it's your turn. It may not be an easy journey—and it won't be a short-term prospect—but it will be worthwhile.

As you are reading the book, go to B2BSocialMedia.com. Oh yeah, we registered the complementary domain to our blog along the way. Seems like the perfect site to support a book called *The B2B Social Media Book*. All the endnotes and examples are on the site and organized by chapter. This way you can easily click for more details about reference materials and company examples. While you are there, subscribe to our regular updates to stay informed on the most recent B2B social media trends.

We have a second offer for you. Go to B2BWorkbook.com for a companion workbook to take the lessons from this book even further. If you want to learn to work even smarter, we have more information and guidance for you. Go get the workbook now!

We held back on offers for so long and they just keep coming. Join an exclusive group of B2B marketers who are willing to stand up and call themselves superstars. Go to B2BSuperStars.com to sign up for access to exclusive webinars, bonus material, and the ability to collaborate with other B2B superstars.

And finally, thank you. Whether you have been following our blog since the early days or you bought this book without having heard of SocialMediaB2B.com, we really appreciate you letting us share these ideas with you.

We would love to hear what you think about our approach to social media lead generation. Please use #B2BSM whenever you mention the book online. This will let us easily find references to it, and will also start to link common conversations about B2B social media. And we definitely want to hear about your transformation into a marketing superstar. Please reach out to us and let us know how you liked the book.

We would also appreciate if you shared a review of the book on Amazon (http://amzn.to/b2bsm2).

Thank you!

—**Kipp Bodnar**
twitter.com/kippbodnar
linkedin.com/in/kippbodnar

—**Jeffrey L. Cohen**
twitter.com/jeffreylcohen
linkedin.com/in/jeffreylcohen

PART

I

The Fundamentals of Social Media Lead Generation

Why B2B Is Better at Social Media Than B2C

Be a marketing superstar. It isn't any more difficult than being ordinary. As a business-to-business (B2B) marketer, you are a core contributor to the growth and success of your company. It is your hard work, balancing the demands of generating quality leads on a limited budget that helps fuel the sales team. Unfortunately, this hard work and diligence often goes underappreciated.

Seventy-three percent of chief executive officers (CEOs) believe marketers are not able to demonstrate how their strategies and campaigns help increase their organizations' top line in terms of more customer demand, sales, prospects, conversions, and market share. This is according to the "2011 Global Marketing Effectiveness Program"[1] by Fournaise Marketing Group.

End this false perception today!

B2B social media marketing is a new set of marketing tools that integrates with existing marketing strategies to help you work smarter instead of harder. When done well, social media marketing can reduce marketing expense, increase lead volume, and provide a clear and measurable return on investment for your marketing dollars. Don't fall victim to the marketing status quo.

The Marketing Status Quo

For decades, B2B marketers would start the year off with a marketing budget and then divide it among print publications, industry trade shows, and some direct mail campaigns. This process involved renting attention from someone else. Renting is expensive.

B2B marketing of the past has been about writing checks for fun ideas and interrupting potential customers with cold calling or direct mail. Enough is enough.

Today's marketing should be about delivering measurable results for the business.

B2B marketing is at a crossroads. You, the marketer, now stand in the face of the most empowering moment of your career. It doesn't matter if you are the chief marketing officer (CMO) or if you have just started your first job in marketing. This is your opportunity to be great at the career you love. Let business-to-consumer (B2C) marketers worry about coming up with the cute mascots.

What Your Marketing Could Be

Marketing greatness is at your fingertips. Open your hand and grab it. Tomorrow is a day in which B2B marketing attracts the best and brightest minds in business. Social media has ushered in a new tool set that complements the skills of B2B marketers more closely than any marketing innovation ever. This book will empower you with the social media tactics, keen content creation insights, data analysis, and reporting methods that will take you to a level of B2B marketing that few CEOs could even imagine.

B2B companies are better suited for social media marketing than B2C companies.

Stop. Go back. Read the last sentence again. It is true.

In the initial adoption of social media marketing, an unfortunate phenomenon happened. It become widely accepted that social media marketing was applicable only to B2C companies. This stereotype ignores five key ways in which social media marketing is better suited for B2B companies. If your boss questions why your B2B company should be using social media for marketing, simply share these five reasons with him or her.

Five Reasons B2B Companies Are a Better Fit for Social Media Marketing Than B2C Companies

1. *Clear Understanding of Customers*—Even more so than B2C marketers, B2B marketers are closely tuned to the behavior, habits, and

desires of their prospects and customers. B2B marketers go far past demographic data. As a B2B marketing superstar, you have clear and detailed personas for every prospect you are working to reach. Having this level of familiarity and clarity is a major advantage in social media marketing.

2. *Depth of Subject Matter Expertise*—B2B companies are trailblazers. They develop new industries or innovate in existing ones. This type of leadership and disruption traditionally means that B2B companies' employees are the leading experts within a particular industry. Because social media is often used as a platform for educating prospects through content and relationships, having the depth of knowledge is a clear boost in the quest for social media marketing success.

3. *Need for Generating Higher Revenue with Lower Marketing Budgets*— You are a miracle worker. You generate leads and brand recognition for your company sales team with a short-handed staff and less budget than you really need. B2B marketers are always looking for value on a quest to maximize cost per lead. Social media acts as a lever to help reduce cost per lead and enables you to do more with less.

4. *Relationship-Based Sales*—The B2B sales process is all about relationships. With large purchase prices and lengthy sales cycles, building strong relationships with sales leads is critical. The social web facilitates relationship building throughout the sales and marketing cycle to help improve lead quality and reduce sales cycle length.

5. *Already Have Practice Doing It*—B2B marketers have long been social media marketing pioneers, even though they might not have known it. Long before the social web, you were publishing newsletters, quarterly magazines, and other marketing tactics that map to many key social media marketing methods. B2B marketers have a history of telling business-focused stories and educating customers with content.

Don't believe us?

Then believe a shipping logistics company that *increased overall quote requests by 270 percent* using social media and inbound marketing. Lynden, Inc. (www.lynden.com), a transportation and logistics company that operates in some of the most remote areas of the world, has leveraged blogging, search engine optimization (SEO), and landing pages to increase quotes for their service online by 412 percent. These results seem astounding, so how did they do it?

Lynden has been blogging since 2009 and creating content to attract new website visits from search engines and social media channels. They use the data and performance from past blog posts to optimize and increase the performance of future content they create. They also track new inbound links that are created as a result of their blog posts and how they rank for specific keywords related to their business.

When Social Media Isn't Right for B2B

This book isn't about sugarplums and gumdrops. Don't think of it as some idealized view of marketing. Instead, it is meant to serve as a reference, inspiration, and a compass for B2B marketers looking to improve and help drive more revenue for their business. Because this book isn't another sugar-coated glamorization of social media, it is important early on to cover situations in which social media marketing *isn't* right for a B2B company.

In these situations some aspects of social media could work and help support other inbound marketing objectives such as search and branding, but the truth is, when it comes to driving transactions, there are better options.

Do you answer yes to any of these questions?

Does your company have fewer than five potential customers? In the B2B space, some companies exist that have an extremely small niche. They fill a need by providing a product or service for only a handful of customers. When your customer base is so targeted, you have to be direct with your limited marketing budget. Regular face-to-face meetings, customer events, and other tactics are a better fit for this niche. Social media helps individuals and companies scale their social interaction. However, when your scale is small, you are less dependent on the scale that social media can provide.

Do purchasing decision makers spend all of their time behind a highly secure firewall? In situations in which you provide products or services to the military, electrical power grid, and others, key purchasing decision makers spend their time in a work environment that is secure and locked down from access to most or all of the information available online. If this is the case for your customer base, then using the Web won't be a successful spend of your marketing budget. The success and engagement of social media depends on the ability to reach and connect with customers digitally and in person. For companies in this environment, the digital option should be a lower priority.

Is your company missing an internal advocate for social media? Sometimes it is not about your customers, but rather, about your organization. One thing that successful organizations have in common when it comes to leveraging social media and word-of-mouth effectively is that they have buy-in from key advocates within the company. At many companies it is the CEO, but at least it is a key decision maker within the organization who can supply the needed resources and leadership to allow the organization to be successful. If you don't have this, then spend your time finding someone within your organization who can fill this role instead of rolling out a social media effort prematurely.

Does your company need to generate a high volume of short-term sales? Can social media drive sales? Yes. Can it drive targeted short-term high-volume sales? In most cases, it cannot. If you have a plan to sell *x* number of units of a product over the next three to four weeks, then social media isn't the right choice for you. As Chris Brogan, coauthor of the book *Trust Agents* says, creating transactional opportunities on the Web takes trust, but trust takes time to establish. If you don't have time, then you must go a different route. These are most likely direct response, pricing incentives, or enhanced sales support.

Does your company have the resources to be successful? A major issue with social media is that most people think that since most online platforms are free, it should be cheap to add social media to their marketing or communications mix. It isn't cheap. Social media marketing done properly takes a lot of time and the support of staff who understand the business of their customers. Many organizations now are simply letting social media happen as an experiment. The problem with this is that, most of the time, these experiments are drastically underresourced and handicapped from the beginning. Understanding the resources that you need and having them in place is a critical factor for success. *Hint:* You will always need more time and money than you expect for executing your social media tactics.

We are not saying that companies in the situations outlined here, can't use social media for their B2B organizations. Instead, we suggest that for these opportunities, there are better ways to leverage the limited pool of resources available and social media should be lower on the priority list.

B2B Social Media as an Annuity

The social web is not linear. Information and interactions happen across the social web in every direction. There is not one clear path. It is critical to understand this simple idea of a nonlinear communications channel. It is this idea that allows you and your organization to begin to think of marketing as an asset, instead of an expense. In the status quo world of marketing where B2B marketing is about renting eyeballs and writing checks, it is easy to view marketing as an expense. In a B2B social media world, marketing is an annuity.

According to Wikipedia, an annuity is used in finance theory to refer to any terminating stream of fixed payments over a specified period. B2B social media marketing functions as a marketing annuity. It delivers website visits, leads, and customers over time, long after the work and budget for the social media tactic have become a distant memory.

Unlike a financial annuity, social media's annuity isn't fixed. Instead, it is compounding. Each tactic stacks on top of the other for exponential results over time. Your management team understands annuities. Help them understand how your marketing budget can become one.

Results Independent of Effort

In traditional outbound B2B marketing such as direct mail and print advertising, 1 + 1 always equals 2. This is because you distribute an interruptive message for a fixed period. In today's marketing world, a marketer budgets to support a company blog post. The output of results from the blog is not limited to a single day or even a fixed amount of time. Heck, it isn't even limited to blogging. Search engine optimization and other inbound marketing tactics benefit as well. A major distinction here is the shift from renting to owning attention, because as a B2B marketer, you own and control your business blog.

Each and every article you publish has an infinite life span. An article you publish today has the potential to have a much larger compounded reach long-term than any initial promotion may have when it is first published. The reason for this is the $1 + 1 = 3$ value of social media. Because a business owns its blog, it is likely to invest in promoting and marketing the blog long term to build an audience. This means that the potential pool of readers for each article is always increasing—to infinity, and beyond!

In addition, every topic and idea has an adoption curve. People seek and consume ideas at different times as they have new business problems to solve.

Annuities Facilitate Scale

Every business has goals. Marketing is a key driver of business revenue and the actualization of the overall growth of the business. The problem with traditional B2B marketing has been that scaling business growth has been completely dependent on spending more money, since many results had an assumed fixed cost. However, as B2B marketing shifts to social media and results become more like annuities, scale isn't a function of marketing budget spend. Instead, scale becomes about consistency and efficiency. Taking actions such as consistently publishing blog content over time or building a LinkedIn Group, serve as an annuity to drive progressively larger results month after month.

Social Media Is Only One Piece

Social media isn't a silver bullet. Many consultants and marketing agencies would like marketers to believe that social media is a magic tonic to solve marketing problems. The truth is that social media isn't a cure-all. Instead, it is one piece of a well-planned and executed inbound marketing strategy that is tightly aligned to business objectives.

In this book when we discuss "business objectives" for marketers, we are talking about lead generation and sales. Although marketing can have other functions, lead generation is the fuel that helps a successful business grow and can speed your trip to marketing superstardom.

Integration wins! Great B2B marketers must solve for integration in every aspect of their work. Social media marketing results are amplified when integrated with e-mail marketing, event marketing, pay-per-click advertising, and other inbound marketing tactics that can be combined to maximize lead generation.

Building a Next-Generation B2B Marketing Team

Marketing superstars in the social media marketing world are incredible hybrids of many communications and business skills. Outbound marketing needed marketers who could set strategy, manage trade shows, work with an advertising agency, and deal with vendors. Notice something important missing in the job description of marketers in the past: customers. None of the skills directly solved the problem of understanding and working with customers.

Social media marketing injects customers directly into the marketing process, where they can accelerate or extinguish marketing efforts. Customers have moved front and center because the social web has democratized publishing. Anyone can publish information today. The cost and barrier to entry in publishing is almost zero. In this book, we will talk at length about leveraging the social web. One thing that should be clear is that the B2B marketing team of the future looks vastly different.

Storytelling + Data Analysis = Great Social Media Marketer

Marketers have historically come from varied educational backgrounds, with journalism and business schools leading the pack. The problem is that great marketers today need a mix of many skills. Great writing skills have long been a requirement for marketers, but being a great writer is no longer enough. A great B2B marketer today should be able to tell stories like an investigative journalist and be able to plow through pivot tables like an investment banker.

Marketing metrics are easier to track online. With automated tracking and data gathering come opportunities to analyze data to uncover ways to optimize and improve marketing results. However, there is nothing to optimize unless the marketing team has created and distributed interesting and engaging content. Think of a great B2B social media marketer as a brand journalist who can also crunch numbers to maximize the results of lead generation offers and calls-to-action. Don't waste time looking for someone who knows how social media tools work. Instead, hire someone who has used social media to deliver quantifiable results. We will get into more detail about building and running a great next-generation marketing team in Chapter 14.

The Perfect B2B Marketing Leader

A great B2B marketing team is only as good as its leader. The job of a top-notch B2B CMO has both drastically changed and stayed the same. A CMO needs to be strategic and have a strong understanding of the industry and the business. In addition, in an online marketing world, a CMO needs to be great at marketing metrics and making strategic investment choices. However, there is one attribute—essential in today's social media marketing world—that many CEOs may overlook: no fear of failure.

With the hurdles into publishing and sharing information now so low, it is harder than ever before for a company to stand out. A great CMO needs to take risks and try new things, while also ensuring that the entire marketing team understands that risk and polarization are accepted and encouraged for the success of the business.

You are the star. Now that we have introduced some important B2B social media principles, it is time to learn all about social media lead generation.

This book is designed to be highly actionable. In order to turn every chapter into actionable marketing activities, we have included a three-step to-do list at the end of each chapter. You should do them. And you need your laptop. They are for your own good. Ready? Go!

Three B2B Social Media Steps to Superstardom

1. *Rally for support*—Any business effort fails without financial and management support. Use the key arguments from the section on why B2B companies are a better fit for social media than B2C companies to build a brief presentation. Your presentation should consist of no more than five clear and concise slides with data. Use this presentation to build internal support for social media marketing within your company.
2. *Integrate social media and traditional marketing*—Remember that social media is only one piece. Integrating marketing is always

more effective than taking a segmented approach. Examine both your social media and traditional marketing strategies and tactics. Schedule a two-hour block of time to look for integration points that connect your social media strategy, such as including links to your social media account on your direct mailings.

3. *Build a winning team*—It doesn't matter what part of your marketing career you are in; you can shape the direction of your marketing team. Push for interview questions and criteria that involve both storytelling and data analysis. When your company has an open marketing position, take 10 minutes to look through your LinkedIn contacts to determine whether you know anyone who has the right skills for the job. If you do, invite that person to interview.

Five-Step Social Media Lead Generation Process

Social media marketing isn't about hugs, kisses, rainbows, or any other fluffy happy words that come to mind. For business-to-business (B2B) companies looking to grow their business, social media marketing is about one thing: leads. Leads are the lifeblood and success metric for every B2B marketing superstar. Leads serve as a foremost indicator of sales. Understanding the full online sales cycle from visit to sale (more on this in Chapter 4) allows you to see your entire marketing strategy in a brand new way.

This chapter's sole focus is leads. We are going to give you all the information you need to generate leads with social media. It isn't as hard as many "experts" say. Instead, we have condensed everything you need to know about social media lead generation into five simple steps.

Before we get into the five steps of social media lead generation, it is important that we define a lead. Businesses define leads differently. Marketing and sales must have a clear and shared agreement on that definition. A lead is someone who raises his or her hand—a person who demonstrates interest in something that a business has to offer.

The information exchanged by the lead prospect, like an ebook or webinar, is the most debated portion of defining a lead. A lead isn't an e-mail address. Blog subscribers or e-mail newsletter subscribers have not yet raised their hands high enough, but they could!

For the purpose of this book, a lead is someone who provides the requested information for a piece of educational content, sales consultation, product demonstration, or offer closely related to a business's product or service. The minimum information required for a lead is a name, company, e-mail address, and phone number. As a marketer, it is your job to test asking for additional relevant information. Asking for more information can help when grading lead quality and make life easier for the sales team. Conversely, having too many fields on a landing page can lower your conversion rate and overall volume of leads.

Step 1: Get the Basics Right

Generating leads using social media starts with three core elements that are the linchpin for the entire online lead generation process: offers, calls to action (CTAs), and landing page. The offer can range from an educational webinar or ebook to a free consultation with a salesperson. CTAs serve as advertisements that businesses use to send visitors to their landing page.

Think of a landing page as an information transaction. Your business provides some type of information and in exchange a visitor to that page provides some of their contact information. Landing pages traditionally do not have any site navigation and have only one goal: lead generation. Landing pages are pages of a business website that contain a form into which visitors can submit information in exchange for an offer.

Secrets to High-Converting Landing Pages

The conversion rate of a landing page is the percentage of visitors who complete and submit the form on the page divided by the total number of visitors to that page. Generating leads with social media can be increased in two ways. The first is by increasing the amount of traffic to a landing page. The second is to increase the conversion rate of a landing page to enable more of the visitors to become leads. Although improving conversion rates for a landing page is a long-term task, following best practices will help you start out with higher conversion rates and more leads.

Landing pages are different from website pages. Most of the pages on a business website are about education. Landing pages are about action. When a person visits a landing page, the most important aspect of the entire page is that it clearly directs the visitor to take an action. For B2B companies that action is to fill out a form in exchange for an offer.

When looking at a landing page, take a step back from the computer. Take a quick glance, really only a second. During that oh-so-brief time and from that further distance, is the action that should be taken on that page clear? Simplicity is key to many aspects of social media marketing, but most important when it comes to landing pages.

Go Naked

Part of creating simplicity on landing pages is removing options for the user. When talking about landing pages, *going naked* refers to removing the navigation of the website from the page in an effort to remove choices and improve clarity for the visitor. It is important to understand that providing too many choices is a bad thing. The more choices you include on a landing page, the higher the likelihood that the site visitor will do nothing and simply leave the page without becoming a lead.

Minimize form length. Reducing friction is key to increasing conversion rates. No, this isn't high school science class where reducing friction is about adding WD-40 to a squeaky door. Reducing marketing friction is about removing any barriers that can stop a visitor from taking the desired action. One of the simplest ways to reduce friction is to reduce the number of fields on a form. The number of form fields is an elegant dance between maximizing leads and providing sales with the information they need. Review each field within a form to determine whether it is important to the sales process. If the answer is no, remove the field from the form.

Offers That Rock

Rock stars sell out arenas because they provide amazing content to their fans in the form of music, live spectacle, and an emotional connection. Part of creating the best B2B lead generation offers is to think like an artist and entertainer. The content of your offer is your art.

A major factor of a landing page's conversion rate is how awesome the offer is. If an offer is truly compelling, the number of form fields and other landing page best practices become less important. The best offers solve a problem for the prospect. For example, a sheet metal roofing company could provide a free calculator that allows prospects to quickly and easily determine the amount of materials they will need for a project. This free calculator could then be placed behind a landing page for lead generation.

Rocking B2B offers should do three things well. The middle chapters of this book are dedicated to getting into the specifics of content creation and distribution. Until then, follow this checklist to ensure offers help drive high conversion rates. Does your offer:

1. Solve a problem for the prospect?
2. Align with the product or service of the business?
3. Provide unique information not easily found in other online resources?

Think Like a Publisher

Most media companies rely on advertising as a revenue source. On the social web, every company is a media company. To maximize business results, marketers should step into the shoes of publishers. The publishing industry has done much of the heavy lifting when it comes to understanding best practices for advertisements (CTAs for us in the B2B marketing world). However, marketers have slightly different needs than traditional publishers.

Most media companies work to maximize page views and advertisement clicks. What this focus ignores is who is clicking on the ads. As a B2B marketer, the most important part in leveraging CTAs for lead generation is solving for who is seeing and clicking on the CTAs. Although an online magazine doesn't care if the same person comes back each day and clicks on an ad, you should.

Content Isn't King; Context Is King

Context drives click-through rates for CTAs. Social media content such as blog posts, tweets, and LinkedIn shares act as social primers. When people look at social primers, they get a bite-sized piece of information on a subject that matters to their business. Having CTAs and offers that are closely aligned in subject matter with the content being shared on social media provides prospects with a way to easily go from introductory content to in-depth subject matter expertise. The more in-depth content customers or prospects consume, the further down the buying cycle they move.

When thinking about CTAs, think about two groups of people: website visitors who still need to be converted to a lead and leads who need to be moved further through the buying cycle. Although both are important, this section focuses on increasing the visitor-to-lead conversion rate of the first group.

B2B marketers need to focus on sending new unique visitors to their content and CTAs on a daily basis. Constantly working to find new visitors is hard. However, social media is a discovery mechanism. Think about how tools such as Facebook and Twitter work. For example, on Facebook, when you comment on or like an article on a company's Facebook Page, that comment, as well as the article from that business, may be shown to other people in your network. Discovery is in the DNA of social media platforms. It is the online way companies such as LinkedIn and Facebook can continue to grow. Social media sharing is crucial to driving more new online leads for your business.

Build Social Media Reach

Landing pages, offers, and CTAs are the foundation of social media lead generation. So is building reach on your different social media platforms. We talk in detail about building reach in Chapter 5. However, it is important to note here that building reach in social media starts with an action. For example, to get more Twitter followers, you have to take the action to find and follow like-minded Twitter users via Twitter Search. The majority of this book is about building and extending social media reach, because it is important to understand that having a community to actually see your content is vital to generating leads with social media.

Step 2: Maximize Content Discovery

Great content has business value only if it is used and consumed by website visitors and leads. As a marketer, one of the most challenging parts of online lead generation can be getting your content seen and shared by others. Scaling social media lead generation and reducing cost of customer acquisition depend on leveraging others to spread your content. Maximizing content discovery can be done by producing awesome content and reducing fiction around sharing that content.

Be Remarkable

Remarkable content is simply that. It is content worth making a remark about. Yes, you're right that that sounds cheesy, and it would be if we weren't planning to help you understand what "remarkable" really means in an actionable way. The power of social media is that the remarks made about content are now public and shared with others online. Being remarkable drives traffic and leads for businesses.

According to Google executive chairman Eric Schmidt, more information is created on the Internet in 48 hours today than was created by all humankind from the beginning of time until 2003. That is an astounding fact and one that underlines that we are now operating in a crowded marketing world in which the winners stand out.

The reason many businesses don't produce remarkable content is fear—fear of giving away too much information, fear of saying something wrong, fear of giving competitors an advantage. These were all rational twentieth century fears. In the twenty-first century, these fears are the quickest path to failure.

Try these five strategies for removing fear in favor of being remarkable in your marketing content:

1. *Pick a side*—Publicly, whether in a blog post or social media message, explain why a certain side of an important industry issue is the right side. Do so in a rational and educated way. Taking one side of an issue creates polarization. Examine the last article you shared with a friend. Odds are that it had a polarizing component. Polarizing isn't about being stupid. Instead, it is about showing that your business actually cares about the industry.

2. *Say something new*—Most B2B companies are full of innovation. Marketers should learn some of the new ideas being developed within a business. Using social media platforms, marketers can get real-time feedback on ideas and grow the marketing reach of the business.

3. *Say something old in a new way*—Most industries have many long-held practices and beliefs that guide businesses. Schedule 30 minutes for the marketing team (even if the marketing team is only you) to brainstorm new ways of presenting these ideas. One way would be to change the content format. Turn an old article into a compelling infographic or video. Another possibility is to discuss older principles in a new framework that adds fresh ideas for even more value.

   For example, consider Texas Instruments. A pioneer of B2B innovation on the product side, Texas Instruments also gets it when it comes to social media content. With SMASH IT (http://e2e.ti.com/group/smashit/m/default.aspx), Texas Instruments employees channel Wayne's World and destroy technology products and, in the process, demonstrate Texas Instruments' impact on each product. Showing components in an end product is classic B2B marketing. With SMASH IT, Texas Instruments takes this classic idea and wraps it in a twenty-first century cover.

4. *Talk about remarkable people*—One hallmark of remarkable content is that it often connects to a person who is remarkable. When thinking about educating potential leads, find a connection to influential people in your industry or beyond. Have a content idea that can relate to the Beatles, Lady Gaga, or someone in pop culture? That is remarkable. In addition, interview industry influencers for your blog; this familiarizes them with your business while giving them something they want: added exposure.

5. *Make it easy*—Sometimes it isn't what is said, but instead how it is said that matters. A trademark of remarkable content is that it is easy to consume and share. Some characteristics of easily consumable content are section headers, bullet points, links to additional information, pictures, and mobile device compatibility.

Build Reach Through Sharing

Prospects don't want to hear about your products. They want solutions to their problems.

This simple idea is the one that most companies get wrong when it comes to social media marketing. Generating new leads for your business involves attracting new prospects. Providing solution-based content through social media is a powerful way to build reach for lead generation.

We have dedicated several chapters in this book to discussing the tactical execution of lead generation on platforms that are core to B2B marketers. However, all of these activities, regardless of the platform, will follow a simple framework for success. See our Content Discovery Framework in Figure 2.1.

Regular Content Creation—Have an editorial calendar that outlines the monthly creation and distribution of all lead generation content through social channels: e-mail, blog, Facebook, Twitter, LinkedIn, forums, etc.

Consistent Sharing—Understanding how prospects want to consume information is key. Many people will opt to use one social channel to

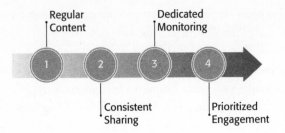

FIGURE 2.1 Content Discovery Framework

consume content from a company. Many social media "experts" will tell you that sharing a piece of content across all social platforms alienates the audience. These experts are wrong. Ask them for their data to support this recommendation. They won't have it. Instead, share lead generation and supporting content across all social channels. However, make sure that the headline or description around the content is customized for the needs and habits of each social community.

Dedicated Monitoring—To optimize and improve social media lead generation, a marketer must be able to collect feedback and iterate. Monitoring social media and using Web analytics tools provide marketers with the feedback they need to improve lead generation month after month. Social media monitoring tools can range from free tools such as Google Alerts (Google.com/Alerts), Twitter Search (Twitter.com/search), and Board Reader (BoardReader.com) to paid tools such as Radian6 (Radian6.com), Alterian (Alterian.com), and CoTweet Enterprise (CoTweet.com). When it comes to analytics, a similar distribution of free and paid tools exist. Google Analytics (Google.com/Analytics) is the leading free Web analytics tool, whereas HubSpot (HubSpot.com) and Omniture (Omniture.com) provide more business-focused analytic data for a fee. Dedicated monitoring doesn't mean having a person who performs only these activities. Instead, it refers to the idea that everyone on a marketing team needs to collect feedback and iterate for each campaign.

Prioritized Engagement—Not every social media mention needs a response. This is a key principal of understanding that many businesses have yet to adopt. All marketing efforts are constrained by the number of people and amount of money available. If you have the time to respond to every social media mentioned, go for it. However, we recommend prioritizing social media engagement on factors such as commenter influence, reach, or dissatisfaction or stage in the buying cycle. Again, this book isn't about blowing bubbles with your customers. It's about generating revenue. Use common sense combined with customer relationship management tools to engage with people who are currently in, or can influence, the sales cycle.

Step 3: Create Conversion Ubiquity

Content is a magnet that pulls prospects closer to becoming sales leads. CTAs and landing pages act like a supermagnet that turns prospects into leads. The lack of conversion opportunities is the single biggest mistake that we see when speaking with B2B marketers working to leverage social media.

Think about the publishing industry. A trade magazine writes an article, then sells advertising alongside those articles, and finally distributes and promotes both the articles and advertisements to its audience. Today, B2B marketers should think of themselves as a vertically integrated publisher. Marketing needs to create content, display CTAs alongside that content, and promote the content to an audience.

Every B2B marketer should have the goal to become the best "trade magazine" for their industry.

However, instead of using costly print formats, marketers should use a blog, e-mail marketing, a LinkedIn Group, a Facebook Page, and a Twitter account. The blog serves as the magazine, and the other channels help promote content and build an audience.

The *New York Times* Is the Competition

Emulate the best, not your competitors. B2B companies are often placed in silos. In strategy meetings, company executives come up with ideas for emulating the best tactics of the competition. Doing this in the age of social media equates to failure. B2B customers aren't robots. The people who sign your multimillion dollar purchase orders read the *New York Times,* buy digital goods from iTunes, and order shoes from Zappos. Aiming to beat a small group of competitors is a formula for failure.

The habits and expectations of B2B customers are being set by major business-to-consumer (B2C) brands. Aim higher the next time you build a marketing strategy. When looking to determine how to improve CTAs on the company blog, don't look to a trade magazine website. Instead, look at the *New York Times* and the *Wall Street Journal*. The survival of these world-class media outlets depends on constantly increasing their advertising revenue both online and offline. Examine what these publications have learned and apply the best ideas to social media marketing CTAs.

Tweeting a Landing Page Doesn't Kill a Puppy

Many social media "experts" would have companies believe that *lead generation* is a dirty word and that it stagnates the growth of building a successful online community. The experts try to convince marketers that sharing a lead generation offer in a blog post, tweet, or Facebook Page update, or through other social media channels, will result in the marketing equivalent of killing a cute and fluffy puppy. These experts are wrong. If you want more proof they are wrong, ask them for data that supports their recommendations.

When doing great social media marketing, many lead generation offers are educationally focused and provide additional insight into an idea. These offers, most often in the form of an ebook or webinar, help solve a prospect's problem. Not sharing educational lead generation offers via social media channels is actually doing a disservice to the online community that the marketing team is working to build and foster. Allow prospects to obtain more in-depth information that can't fit into a tweet, blog post, or Facebook update by sharing lead generation offers in social media.

Step 4: Test and Fail Fast

Iterating is everything. Waiting for perfection is the enemy. The Web is an inherently different medium than print. The Web isn't linear. Users bounce from link to link, instead of flipping through pages. The days of pouring over a layout for hours to make sure no typos exist before the brochure goes to print are over.

One of the most important things a B2B marketer can do is to ship ideas and iterate. By shipping ideas, we mean publish a blog post the same day it was written instead of sending it to 20 people for review. It could also be coming up with a contest for LinkedIn Group members and launching it once budget and rules are approved. If you are a B2B chief marketing officer (CMO) or executive reading this book, please take away this one idea: *Reducing approvals and empowering marketing to ship online content is the single biggest lever you can pull to increase lead generation.*

Iterating allows you to take the most powerful action any marketer can do: Stop marketing that doesn't work. You are too busy. It isn't possible to add more hours in the day. The only way to get more time back for new marketing strategies, such as social media, is to stop strategies and tactics that don't work. Stop now. This simple idea of stopping tactics that don't work will instantly make you a better marketer.

Marketing Tactics Are Lab Rats

Have a methodology for marketing tests. Having a test for all marketing tactics will help ensure a stronger strategy. Testing will also help uncover flawed ideas and tactics earlier in the process, saving valuable time. The hardest part about testing is setting the right framework for the test before it starts. Luckily, we have done a lot of the heavy lifting for you and drafted a framework that we think . . . well . . . kicks ass. See our Social Media Lead Generation Testing Framework in Figure 2.2.

A Kick-Ass Marketing Testing Framework

Note: To demonstrate how this framework would work for your business, we created a hypothetical Facebook contest to use as an example.

Step 1: Set a clear quantitative objective.

Example: If the Facebook contest generates 50 leads and 200 new page likes in 60 days, given the allocated amount of marketing team time and budget, it was successful.

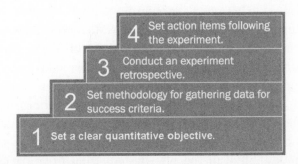

4 Set action items following the experiment.

3 Conduct an experiment retrospective.

2 Set methodology for gathering data for success criteria.

1 Set a clear quantitative objective.

FIGURE 2.2   Social Media Lead Generation Testing Framework

Step 2: Set methodology for gathering data for success criteria.

Example: Use a unique landing page for the Facebook contest to measure leads generated directly from the contest. Look at Facebook's Insights analytics tool to determine total growth in page likes during the 60-day period.

Step 3: Conduct an experiment retrospective.

Example: Gather all team members involved with the experiment for a quick 30-minute discussion. The discussion should include:

What worked?

What didn't work?

What could be improved?

Did the test maintain its original scope?

Step 4: Set action items following the experiment.

Example: If objectives are met, plan a second Facebook contest and expand the percentage of the team's time dedicated to Facebook.

If objectives are not met, reduce the current level of investment in Facebook for lead generation. Evaluate the viability of Facebook again in six months.

This framework isn't absolute. Every business will have its own priorities and issues that may cause this framework to be adjusted. Use this structure as a basis for one that best fits the needs of your business.

If You Aren't Failing, You're Doing It Wrong

Marketing is often about choosing which risks to take. As marketers, we are competitive. We want to be great at the work we do. In order to win, the natural notion is to reduce the risk of a failed marketing effort. Learning to accept failure is one of the single most important things that a marketer can do to become a superstar.

Failure and greatness are oddly linked. Most great innovations at the start have an uncomfortably high perceived risk of failure. Think about all the employees who told Steve Jobs that people wouldn't use a phone that had only one button and a touch screen. The problem with failure and our fear of it is that we rarely take the time to reflect on what birthed a historic innovation. Most often at the start of every major innovation was a core group of people close to the issue predicting its quick and dramatic failure. Think of all of the people who proclaimed that the Internet was "just a fad."

It takes the same amount of effort to be great at something as it does to be only good. The difference between great and good exists in the vision, dedication, decision making, and acceptance of failure that great individuals and teams have.

Think with a Magic Wand

Imagine, as you are about to prioritize your next round of marketing activities, that you have a magic wand. That magic wand removes all roadblocks and ensures perfect execution of your plan. Now that worrying about the details is no longer an issue, thanks to the magic wand, take a minute to think about the results of the plan. If everything went perfectly, how would this idea affect the business? If the answer is a little bit or slightly better than current marketing tactics, then the fear of failure has crept in to the plan. Accepting failure opens you up to potential ideas and strategies that not only can meet the goals of the company but sometimes can far surpass them and transform the economics of the business. Embrace failing. Fail all the way to greatness.

Step 5: Optimize for Maximum Lead Flow

The last step of many good methodologies is kind of a rinse and repeat step. This methodology is no different. The previous four steps of this social media lead generation methodology are designed to provide everything needed to become a lead-generating machine. The fifth step is about amplifying the results and effectiveness of the previous four.

Leads are coming in through social media channels. So, what does the sales team say? "Wow! These new inbound leads are great. Can we get more of them?" This simple question brings both a smile and a tear to marketers everywhere. On one hand, sales trusts marketing and is reducing cold-calling in favor of the awesomeness of prospects raising their hands through social media and inbound channels. On the other hand, this love for inbound leads puts more pressure on the marketing team to deliver.

Uncovering Opportunities for Optimization

When the goal is to increase lead volume, two core levers can be pulled. The first is to drive more traffic to the top of the funnel. The second option is to optimize CTAs and landing pages to maximize the number of visitors who are converted into leads.

We believe that it is always better to start with the second option. By improving the visit-to-lead conversion rate for a website, we can take advantage of all future traffic increases and drive more leads per month. The first part of this process is to establish a benchmark for the landing page conversion rate.

Maximizing Landing Page and Call-to-Action Conversion Rates

Examine the conversion rate (percentage of visitors to that page who completed and submitted the lead form) rate for each of your landing pages. Look at the median conversion rate for all landing pages in an effort to avoid performance outliers. Add 5 percentage points to the median landing page conversion rate. This new number is now the goal conversion rate, often called a benchmark for all current and future landing pages. Optimization is one part art and one part science, but you don't need oil paints and a Bunsen burner. Make adjustments and track them over time to determine best practices for your business to maximize conversion rate. Some items to test include reducing form length, changing the page headline or image location, differing images, and embedding a video.

CTAs can also be tested in the same way. Adjust placement, design, and colors of a CTA image or text to improve its click-through rate. Click-through rate is the number of people who click on the CTA button compared with the total number of people that see the page. By improving click-through rates of CTAs and conversion rates for landing pages, you can boost your visitor-to-lead percentage.

Filling the Top of the Funnel

Web analytics are the key to understanding how to drive more traffic to a website and landing pages. Understanding current and past visitor behavior through Web analytics enables you to prioritize efforts. Log into the Web analytics software for your business. Examine the traffic refers to the website and landing pages. What percentage of them are from search? Social media? Other websites? E-mail marketing?

Review the breakdown of website traffic. Then, dig a layer deeper. What factors are driving traffic from the top sources? It could be a link on a popular site, an e-mail marketing campaign, or something completely different. The objective is to understand what is working and apply that to other channels, with the goal of bringing more traffic to the site.

More than half of this book is about driving traffic to help fill the top of the funnel. Take these ideas along with the ones from future chapters to amplify and build the best social media lead generation process.

Lead generation isn't the bane of a marketer's existence. Instead, it is the fuel that allows you to help build a business, while showing a clear return on investment from marketing strategies. Let this lead generation process help power you to marketing superstardom.

Three B2B Social Media Lead Generation Steps to Superstardom

1. *Build an online lead generation infrastructure*—The rest of this book is useless without this pivotal step. Using the information outlined in Step 1 of the Five-Step Social Media Lead Generation Process, create a set of offers, landing pages, and CTAs related to your product or service. Check out Chapter 6 to learn more about creating great ebooks and webinars.

2. *Implement the four steps of content discovery*—Content is the fuel of social media lead generation. To maximize the return on your content investment, be sure to support *regular content creation* by creating an editorial calendar for your corporate blog with a plan of publishing at least one post per week. Set up automatic publishing from your blog to your social media accounts using tools such as Twitterfeed (Twitterfeed.com) to facilitate *consistent sharing*. Set aside 10 minutes each day for *dedicated monitoring*. Take an additional five minutes to *prioritize engagement* and respond to any important brand or industry mentions.

3. *Start testing*—Testing facilitates iteration and improvement. Set up a test involving one of your social media marketing tactics. Remember to set a clear qualitative objective, set a methodology for gathering data for success criteria, conduct an experiment retrospective, and set action items following the experiment. Testing is all about the numbers. Make sure that at every point of your test, you have quantifiable metrics combined with data collection methods that are as automated as possible.

Yes, Chapter 3 in a Social Media Book Is about Search (It's That Important!)

Don't close the book. No need to check the title. Yes, this is *The B2B Social Media Book,* and yes, the third chapter is about search. There are two reasons for this choice. First, search is at the core of any great business-to-business (B2B) social media strategy. Second, search is in the midst of a social evolution. No marketing channel is an island, especially social media. In marketing, integration always wins. As far as marketing integration opportunities go, search and social media are like peas and carrots. Wait, strike that. Who really eats peas and carrots together? Let's go with a classic. Search and social media are the peanut butter and jelly of the online marketing world.

Evolution of Search

When search started, it wasn't much more than a digital Yellow Pages, without the killing of trees and the heavy lifting. The problem that search tried to solve when online search engines first launched has remained the same: to provide users with the answers they are looking for as quickly as possible.

Context as the Foundation of Search

The first search engines (remember Lycos?) really used only one factor to judge which Web page could best answer a question: context. Keywords and the density of those keywords on a page were the information that search engines used to return results to users. Today, these techniques are called on-page search engine optimization (SEO). Although context was the dominant original search engine factor, it is now only a piece of the puzzle in increasing organic search traffic.

Think of yourself as a translator. You are trying to translate the theme, knowledge, and information of your company website into a format that search engines can understand. As a marketer it is important to take advantage of every opportunity to give search engines a clear understanding of the content on each page of a website. These optimization opportunities are not the only ways to point search engines in the right direction, but they are the most important and most often neglected.

Four On-Page Optimization Opportunities

1. *URL Structure*—Search engines look at the words that are in a URL of a Web page. Too often this text goes unoptimized, or even worse, doesn't exist. Ever gone to a website and seen a page like this: exampledomain.com/132? Using numbers as the URL for Web pages is the default setting in many content management systems. The correct way to optimize a Web page to increase search engine traffic is exampledomain.com/target-keyword. If you sold construction equipment to manufacturers as one of your products, you would want the URL text of that product page to include your targeted keyword for that product: exampledomain.com/manufacturing-construction-equipment.

2. *Page Title*—Look at the top of your Internet browser. Above the entry bar for the URL you will see some text. That text at the top center of your Web browser or on each tab is called the page title. The page title text is also the text that a user sees and clicks on when looking at results in a search engine. The page title is an opportunity for marketers to help search engines better understand the content of the page and to entice search engine users to click on the link. The page title should focus on the same targeted keyword as your URL and page text.

3. *Page Text*—The words you use in the text of a Web page and how often you use them matter. It isn't the core determination for rankings, like it was in the early stage of search engines. Instead it is one of many signals a search engine puts into its ranking algorithm.

FIGURE 3.1   Key Website Optimization Aspects

Be sure to include target keywords in both headers and body text on a page. Don't try to stuff keywords on the page, making the page copy confusing. Search engines are too smart for it. Plus, it hurts your ability to convert visitors to the page into leads. If your copy doesn't sound natural, your keyword density is too high. See Figure 3.1 for a visual explanation of key website optimization aspects.

4. *Meta Description*—The meta description is a 160-character or less description of the page. Some content management systems allow you to easily customize this for every page. Check with your web developers to learn how to do this on your website. When search engines first started, it was an important factor for ranking well. No longer is that the case. The meta description may be a small factor in search engine ranking, but it serves a more important role today. When you use a search engine, the text that is displayed below the link for a search engine result is the meta description for that page. This means the meta description is a huge opportunity for enticing searchers to click the link for your result and visit that page. Focus on writing clear and engaging meta descriptions. Don't bother stuffing them with keywords. See Figure 3.2 for an example of meta description in a search engine result listing.

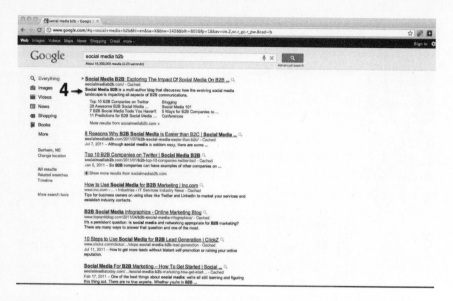

FIGURE 3.2   Meta Description in Search Results

Authority Drives Ranking

It wasn't long before search engines realized that website owners could pack, cram, and jam their sites full of keywords to game the system. Still working to solve the problem of giving the right answer to the right user at the right time, search engines were forced to evolve. Search engines needed some way of determining which site was truly an authority on a subject. The answer to this problem was to combine contextual data with inbound linking data. An inbound link is when one website links to another website. Search engines look at these links as votes to determine which sites should be considered the authority or first search result for a keyword.

Think of a search engine like Google or Bing as a giant peer-review system where journals are replaced by websites and votes are cast with links. As in the academic world, not all votes are equal. If you are a researcher and someone from Harvard validates your research, it will likely have more impact than if the same vote of confidence came from a lesser-known institution. SEO works the same way. Votes from popular and authoritative websites, such as CNN.com and other news websites, government websites, and education websites with .edu domains, are some of the best votes (inbound links) that business websites can secure.

However, when it comes to SEO, both quality and quantity of links matter. The more links, the better. Higher-authority links act like jet fuel to amplify the impact to produce more search traffic in less time.

Three Strategies for Link Building Success

Increasing the quantity and quality of inbound links to a business website is one of the core challenges for online B2B marketers. Although it isn't easy, it pays off in the way of sustainable long-term traffic and leads from search engines. These three strategies should aid in the hunt for inbound links to improve search engine rankings.

1. *Blog*—The single best thing a B2B business can do to increase its traffic from search engines is to have a company blog that is part of the main company website. For example, it could be Blog.YourCompanyDomain.com or YourCompanyDomain.com/Blog. Every blog post is a new opportunity to bring in first-time visitors through search engines and social media. Discussing industry news, as well as mentioning top industry bloggers and publications, is a solid tactic for building targeted inbound links with a business blog. See Chapter 7 to learn how to become a world-class B2B blogger.

   360 Signs (360signs.com/blog=0), a commercial signing company in Austin, Texas, has used blogging to generate more than 500 new inbound links to their website in one year. By creating regular blog content that was targeted at specific keywords and explaining sign industry issues, 360 Signs has increased search engine traffic to their website by more than 700 percent.

2. *Ask Peers and Partners*—A great B2B salesperson will say, "Ask for the close." When it comes to inbound links, salespeople are right. Ask for inbound links. The best place to start building inbound links is with partners and vendors. Look at partner or vendor websites and see how they are currently linking to other businesses. For example, do they have a partner page or recommended vendors page? Identify the best way for your business to be included in their website strategy and ask them for the link. The important part of this process is to help the partner or vendor understand why it is beneficial to give you the link. For example, if it is a vendor and the link is on the company's testimonials page, then it is valuable to that

vendor because you are providing a public recommendation for its product or service.

3. *Build It into Public Relations*—In addition to asking partners and vendors for inbound links, it is also important to get the public relations team in on the link-building action. When the public relations team, whether it is an internal person or an agency, gains coverage about the company, have the team ask for a link to a specific page of the website in the online version of the article. Media sites have some of the highest authority on the Web, so getting an inbound link from one could greatly improve the rank of a Web page. This is why having them link to a specific page of the website, instead of the home page, is so powerful.

Changing Authority

Although links still hold a massive amount of authority for how search engines rank websites, the way search engines are measuring authority is quickly changing. Remember CD players, those clunky things that spun discs that had only 12 songs on them? Google's ranking algorithm today is like a CD player, soon to be replaced by the iPod and on its way to becoming obsolete.

Using inbound links was a huge step forward from the keyword-stuffing early days of search. However, links aren't the best solution for providing the right answer at the right time. First, although they are a good signal of credibility, they aren't updated in real time. Think about how fast information travels today. Search engines need better signals to keep up with us, the searchers. Second, many questions posed in searches are personal. Two people may ask the same question in their searches, but they likely are seeking different answers. The current ranking algorithm used by Google doesn't provide personalized context.

What function like links but are faster and more personal? Social media shares likes, updates, and content. Social media shares and mentions are quickly becoming the new inbound link. Bing, a major search engine, has deals in place with popular social media platforms to access data to display in search results. Do a quick search on Bing and you will find updates from Twitter and Facebook, along with many other social networks, displayed along website links and blog posts.

When Google rolled out its own social network, Google+, in mid-2011 news outlets were heralding it as the next great Facebook competitor.

These writers simply missed the point. Google+ is about maintaining and expanding Google's dominance in the search engine market. Google+ will likely never have as many users as Facebook, but that doesn't matter. The value that Google+ holds is that it is a treasure trove of personalized signals of authority that Google owns and doesn't have to lease from another company that could decide to cut Google off at any moment.

Google's +1 feature and Facebook's Like button are two ways that major Web companies are baiting users to provide more customer data and recommendations for content on the Web. SEOmoz has released data that show a correlation between the number of shares a blog post gets on Facebook to its position in Google's search results. It is this type of data that demonstrates the desire to move away from links as the key determinant in search engines to a more personalized authority based on social connections across online networks.

Social Search and B2B

SEO is the number one reason a B2B company should be using social media marketing. Take a second. Read that sentence again. B2B companies understand that search engines drive valuable qualified traffic to their websites. Many companies are working on SEO efforts to increase this traffic. One of the most important ways to increase search engine traffic is to leverage social media. Social media isn't the first thing a business should focus on to improve search traffic, but it is certainly part of long-term SEO success.

The social web isn't a bunch of silos. Often, marketing experts talk about SEO, social media, e-mail marketing, and so on, as separate channels. Yes, they are different, but they all work together and amplify one another. As we have already talked about, search engines are starting to use signals from social media platforms to rank Web pages. One way to take advantage of this change in authority is to have a unified keyword strategy across SEO and social media marketing.

Unified Keyword Strategy

A keyword strategy is the first thing every B2B company should start working on when beginning both search and social media marketing efforts. A unified keyword strategy is a list of keywords that will be targeted for increasing search engine traffic, social media reach, and influencer engagement. By having one keyword strategy, it enables the amplification of results across search and social media. For example, if you are using the same keywords in social media messages that you are optimizing for search engines, then it amplifies to search engines and to social media followers that your business is an authority on that subject.

For example, take the Ecomagination initiative of General Electric (GE). Their Twitter handle (Twitter.com/ecomagination) frequently tweets about "smart grid" technology as a core term for their business. GE also ranks on the first page of search results in Google for the term *smart grid,* which shows their search and social media keyword strategies are unified.

To build a unified keyword strategy, first start by researching the popularity and competition for keywords specific to your business in search engines. This can be done with Google AdWords' free keyword research tool,[1] as well as with paid tools, including HubSpot (HubSpot.com) and SEOmoz (SEOmoz.com). The major difference between free and paid tools is time savings and additional data. Many free tools can tell you how many people search for a keyword per month. However, they can't examine your business website and tell you where you currently rank for that keyword and how hard it would be to increase that rank.

Once you have a solid list of keywords to focus on from an SEO perspective, then integrate those keywords into your social media engagement efforts. Use free URL tracking tools like bitly, as well as Web analytics, to determine which keywords and content are resonating most in social media. If you have Google Analytics installed on your website, make sure you use campaign codes to precisely track which social media updates and platforms drive website traffic.

Unified Keyword Action Item

Pick five common keywords that relate to your business. Write a blog post for each keyword, using the keyword in the title of each post. Then, share those blog posts on social networks, including LinkedIn, Facebook, and Twitter. Using website analytics software, review the traffic for each article, specifically traffic from social media sites. Looking at this data you can understand how each social media community reacts to each keyword.

By conducting the test from the action item previously discussed, data are created to better prioritize the unified keyword list. It is common to have a large list (500+) of keywords for SEO. A list that large is hard to manage. The 80/20 rule, when used in this case, would say that 80 percent of traffic is going to come from 20 percent of those 500+ keywords. But which 20 percent? This is why having the data from the previous action item is so powerful. Use a series of experiments combined with data on the number of people searching for a keyword to determine which are your best keyword phrases. When search and social media marketing are integrated, social media can be used to prioritize keywords. Finding the right 20 percent of keywords will help accelerate traffic and leads!

Rank Is Dead

The position for which a website ranks for a keyword doesn't matter. Rank is the position of your website compared with competitors' sites and other sites on a search engine's result page for a specific keyword. Many B2B marketers who focus on SEO obsess over where their website ranks for each of their targeted keywords. Don't do it. The reality is that we live in the age of the social web. Online experiences are becoming more personalized and contextual every day. Search is no different. Look at how you shop on sites like Amazon. They know who you are, what you have purchased, and what you have looked at, and they use that information to customize your shopping experience.

Keyword rank is dead for the same reason that Amazon knows you want a new coffee pot. Rank used to be a global item. It was the same for everyone everywhere. Now ranking of search results is based on your previous, personal search history.

Google serves up search results based on what you clicked on whether you are logged in or not. They also use the location you are searching from. Results change if you are in Phoenix or Boston. Google uses the IP address of Internet connections to provide location-focused search results, even if the searcher doesn't include a location in their keyword phrase. Add in other factors such as friends and recommendations from social media, and search becomes closer and closer to shopping at Amazon. This level of customization makes keyword rank irrelevant. It makes social media reach, comments, and shares more important than ever. If you take one thing away from this chapter, it should be this: *For a B2B company to have successful search engine marketing in 2012 and beyond, it must leverage social media.*

Instead of spending hours each week focusing on search engine rank, work on building a community of active sharers of your content on social media. (More on this in future chapters!)

Search Isn't Just Google

While you are still shaking your fist at us for demonstrating why search engine rank is no longer important, we have some other news for you. Google isn't the only search engine. Sure, you know about Yahoo! and Bing. Their share of the search market has grown to a combined 30 percent. Microsoft handles all of the self-service search advertisements on Yahoo!, so as paid search goes, Microsoft has 30 percent of the market. However, Microsoft isn't Google's key concern. As a B2B online marketer, it is critical that you understand a current shift in the search engine industry.

Search is fracturing. Facebook, Yelp, YouTube, Twitter, and LinkedIn have become powerful brokers of data and user searches. The future of search is about understanding that software platforms are becoming colossal data stores. Any company that holds the access to a large amount of interesting data has a card to play in the next round of search evolution. From a B2B standpoint, the industry has had niche search engines such as ThomasNet (ThomasNet.com). However, imagine a world in which Salesforce.com is a search engine. It already is for many sales and marketing professionals for internal company data. But with their launch of Data .com, they are providing access to millions of contacts and company profiles within the platform. It has become a controlled search engine where the results are all signal and no noise. When it comes to search, the key point is to look forward, not back. Forget keyword stuffing and rank.

Embrace the future of search. It is social.

Social search is ripe with opportunities for B2B companies who can encourage customers and partners to connect their word of mouth online and offline. In a world of relationship sales and search engines where information is ranked on relationships, B2B companies have an inherent advantage over their business-to-consumer (B2C) counterparts. Social media and search, when combined, amplify marketing results unlike the integration of most offline tactics.

Three B2B Search Engine Optimization Steps to Superstardom

1. *Build a unified keyword strategy*—This strategy should leverage content and social media to help determine the keywords with the potential to drive the majority of search engine traffic. Filter your SEO keyword list to a unified list of fewer than 50 keywords and develop a strategy for driving more search and social traffic from those 50 keywords in the next six months through blogging and social media sharing.

2. *Drop useless search metrics*—Stop obsessing over keyword rank. Instead, look at the keywords that are driving the most leads and customers. Support these keywords with blog posts, lead generation offers, social media, and other inbound marketing tactics to drive meaningful business results.

3. *Build links*—Links still matter and will continue to matter even though social media will play a larger role in the ranking of search engine results. Follow the three tips for building links outlined in this chapter with the goal of adding 10 new inbound links to your website in the next 90 days. Use OpenSiteExplorer.com to measure your improvement in inbound links.

How to Close the Loop of Social Media ROI

Social media marketing is about generating business-to-business (B2B) leads and revenue. It is not about generating buzz, creating content that goes viral, gaining positive mindshare, or using any other fluffy metric. Marketing's job is to contribute to revenue generation, not be a cost center for superficial activities with no clear return on investment (ROI).

Determining the ROI of social media marketing isn't some mythic quest that starts with you riding off on a white horse. It is actually much clearer than the ROI of many offline marketing efforts. This is the beauty of the Web. Actions are trackable. Social media marketing is measurable. You just need to understand what to measure.

Warning: This chapter contains math.

Being great at math and data analysis are keys to becoming a successful marketing superstar. We will weave strategies, theory, and math in an attempt to demystify B2B social media marketing ROI.

Before we go any further, let's talk about access to your company's financial data. If you work for a transparent company where you see monthly sales reports and marketing expenses, you are a-okay for the chapter ahead. But if you work for a company where financial data is available only via court order, you need to pause right now and set up a meeting with your supervisor, or whoever can authorize your access to this information. After reading this chapter, get this person in authority to read this chapter. Tell him or her that you want to show the ROI and that *The B2B Social Media Book* says you need this information. Put your finger right here and say, "Look, it says right here that this is what we need to do."

$$\frac{[\text{TLV} - \text{COCA}]}{\text{COCA}} = \text{ROI}$$

FIGURE 4.1 Social Media ROI Formula

The Math of ROI

As demonstrated in Figure 4.1, measuring the ROI of an overall B2B marketing team or even a single B2B campaign is a simple math problem. It is gathering the numbers to execute the math that is the challenge. To determine the ROI of any B2B marketing effort, follow this simple formula. (Note: This formula is to give you ROI as a percentage.)

$$\frac{[\text{Total lifetime value (TLV)} - \text{Cost of customer acquisition (COCA)}]}{\text{COCA}} = \text{ROI}$$

This simple formula is what separates good marketers from great ones—because although it is a simple problem to compute, the devil lies in the details of accurately calculating TLV and COCA.

Calculating COCA

COCA is the "I" in ROI.

COCA is all of the costs required to bring a customer in the door. This makes COCA typically a sales and marketing metric. To calculate COCA, add all marketing costs, including salaries and overhead of team members, outside agency costs, and contractor costs, and all paid advertising for a set period of time, whether it is a month, quarter, or year.

The next step is to combine all sales-related costs, such as commissions, operations costs, and other sales-related expenses, to understand the full COCA for your business. This number can then be divided by the revenue attributed to these marketing and sales efforts during the time you are measuring to determine the COCA per customer. When looking to determine the ROI of marketing by channel instead of the aggregate efforts, it is important to determine the COCA per channel.

For example, let's say one of your marketing team members spends half of her time writing and editing the company blog. Her monthly salary is $3,000. Divide that monthly salary in half, $1,500; she only spends half of her time on the blog. Salary is only part of the cost. You have overhead costs that come with every employee and that normally averages between 40 and 50 percent. Let's err on the high side and say this employee's overhead is 50 percent. Take 50 percent of $1,500, which gives you an additional $750 for overhead cost. Then you need to determine any hard costs for operating your blog, such as hosting, design, or any other maintenance. For the sake of this example, let's say that your monthly costs for your blog are $100. So, when you combine the costs—salary ($1,500) + employee overhead costs ($750) + technical costs ($100)—you get a monthly marketing blog COCA of $2,350.

Knowing your sales cycle is critical when reporting COCA and ROI. For example, it is June 30 and the objective is to determine the ROI from the first two quarters of marketing efforts. Let's say that this B2B company has a sales cycle of 90 days. This means that, on average, it takes 90 days for a lead generated by marketing to become a customer. Because of the sales cycle, it is possible for this company to determine the ROI for only the first quarter of marketing efforts and not the second. Any lead generated after April 1 is less than 90 days old, the average sales cycle, so reporting customers for the leads generated after April 1 would be prematurely reporting revenue generated from the second quarter marketing investment.

Accurate budgeting and reporting are important components of a successful marketing team and are the core success factors in understanding COCA for a business.

Understanding Total Lifetime Value

TLV is the "R" in ROI.

TLV is the average amount of revenue paid to a business by a customer over the lifetime of the relationship. To have an accurate understanding of the TLV for your business, you will need to be close buddies with your financial team. TLV is about clearly understanding your business model. The first component of TLV is the value of an average sale.

For example, let's consider a textile manufacturer that sells reams of fabric to clothing companies. On average, each ream costs $40. A typical customer buys 1,000 reams. This makes the average sale for the business $40,000.

Wait. The average sale amount is not TLV. It ignores one important aspect of a business: repeat purchasing. To understand TLV, you need to understand not only your average sale amount but also how many sales are made to one customer over the entire lifetime of a customer, aka your customer retention rate.

TLV depends largely on the type of business. A B2B manufacturer that sells electrical transformers may have a high average sale and a loyal customer base, but the product could have a long life span, such as 10 years. This lengthy product life span is a factor that lowers the TLV, since the customer won't be making many return purchases. Conversely, if a company sells commercial-grade paper products, such as bathroom towels, the TLV would be primarily driven by the sales team's ability to lock customers into long-term purchase contracts.

Making money is fun. Understanding how much an average company pays your business is even more fun. It helps the entire company understand the value of their work and makes the results of your marketing efforts clearer.

LESSONS FROM A MARKETING SUPERSTAR

Name: Pam O'Neal
Title: Vice President of Marketing
Company: BreakingPoint Systems, Inc.
Years in Current Position: 3.5
What is your greatest social media/marketing success?
Using blog content to attract a loyal following of motivated buyers. Specifically, I would point to the popularity and revenue contribution of the BreakingPoint Systems and NetQoS blogs. In my experience a good technology blog offers the best avenue for B2B marketers in emerging companies to capture interest, educate buyers, and generate actionable leads.

At BreakingPoint, our blog is a strategic companywide initiative that drives top placement in search engines, attracts a loyal following, converts readers to buyers, and facilitates ongoing communication with customers. The high-value content contributed by everyone in the company helps us build a reputation for helping customers and prospects solve urgent problems. It then provides the added benefit of driving our search engine ranking higher on issues our customers are researching.

Our CRM dashboard and Web analytics clearly show a link between our social media programs and triple-digit revenue growth at BreakingPoint. In fact, we've closed millions of product sales from inbound Web leads over the past two years for an ROI of 2,800 percent! How often do you see that in B2B marketing programs these days?

Plus, the snowball effect of the accumulated blog content means we are seeing a steady increase in search-driven Web traffic and actionable leads with no end in sight. We've tracked a 14 percent increase in Web traffic and an 18 percent increase in conversion of Web traffic to leads in the past six months.

It's also important to note that our blog serves other important functions at BreakingPoint, including market education and thought leadership. In the test industry, we don't have many opportunities for coverage in trade magazines. Using the fresh and relevant content on the blog, we are able to push out frequent updates to thousands of Twitter and LinkedIn followers as well as an emerging Facebook fan base. Our blog and growing social media following have been critical in helping us start meaningful online discussions about testing that are truly changing the market.

Lessons Learned

1. Engage and incentivize everyone in your company to develop blog content.
2. Spread the same content far and wide. Post in a variety of formats to SlideShare, YouTube, LinkedIn, Facebook, PitchEngine, and as many locations as possible. Don't forget the inbound links.
3. Update and add offers to old blog posts. Google has no expiration date, and it's far easier to edit old posts than to write new ones.

(continued)

(*continued*)

4. Use Web analytics and lead tracking to demonstrate the value of your efforts. Share this with all of your writers to encourage them to contribute more.
5. Post stats highlighting top-performing content to foster healthy competition. I always enjoy watching marketing versus engineering posts.

What is your biggest roadblock in executing your social media strategy? At NetQoS it was executive buy-in. However, that was not the case at BreakingPoint for two reasons. First, the executive team knew it would take this type of direct, "nonmarketing" approach to reach our buyers. More important, the NetQoS success demonstrated it was possible to drive revenue growth using social media techniques. Demonstrating results is really the key with any marketing program. By tracking our ongoing contribution with the BreakingPoint blog, we were able to secure funding to develop a customer keyword-driven blog and pay a small bounty to writers to increase our technical content.

What is the single most important trait of a B2B marketer? There was a time that I would have said *empathy,* but these days I'm beginning to think *fearlessness* is the key. You have to jump in with both feet and capture the opportunity at hand. Then watch the response and adjust your approach if necessary. The point is, you cannot wait around to get approval while a great opportunity passes you by. With sound judgment and a revenue-driven mind-set the chances are good that your efforts will deliver value.

Social Media Is Good for COCA and TLV

Two key metrics for improving any B2B company are decreasing COCA and increasing TLV. Well, yeah, that makes sense. Make more money while spending less. How can marketing help? Traditionally, the only metric that marketers could affect has been COCA, which they were able to help reduce. However, social media puts us in a situation that we have never been in before. It is now possible for a marketing team to positively impact COCA *and* TLV.

Marketing superstars can reduce cost and increase revenue.

For most marketers, the first step in reducing COCA is to increase the number of leads coming from organic sources (direct traffic, organic search, social media, referrals from other websites, etc.). Leads from organic sources have a lower cost per lead. Remember, with organic channels, we own the attention, but with paid channels, we are merely renting. Generating more organic leads often means a reduction in paid media spending. Reducing paid media is a speedy way to drive that ugly COCA number down.

Social media acts like an annuity to drive exponentially more traffic and leads over time when done properly. Unlike paid lead generation sources who stop sending leads once the invoices are paid, social media's annuity benefits can help drive COCA lower and lower, quarter after quarter.

As marketers we understand that it is our job to reduce COCA, but how can we improve TLV? Social media is a different type of marketing. Instead of interrupting customers with clever magazine ads or charming cold calls, it relies on education. Successful B2B social media marketing is fueled by content that teaches prospects about industry best practices, trends, and solutions from your business that help support these best practices. The end result is a prospect that is better educated than ever before about the products he or she is buying and the problems these products help to solve. More educated customers have a head start on their path to being happier and more loyal customers. The increase in loyalty is key for improving TLV by influencing more return purchases.

One reason social media must be part of a B2B marketing plan is because it is one of the few strategies that can positively impact COCA *and* TLV.

Intent Is Attribution

Before anyone can measure ROI, he or she first needs to understand what is being measured and have a method for data collection in place. When it comes to ROI, one of the key choices that has to be made is attribution. To understand which leads and customers were generated through social media sources, a method for attributing that lead and customer to social media or another marketing source must exist.

First- versus Last-Action Attribution

When thinking about attribution, two major schools of thought exist: first-action attribution and last-action attribution. In the method of first-action attribution, a lead and customer are attributed to a marketing source when that customer first visits the company website from that source. A marketing source is essentially the referrer to the website. The source could be a Facebook post, a pay-per-click advertisement, a direct mail piece, a search engine, etc.

Let's consider a marketing funnel example:

User clicks a link on Twitter → reads a blog post → signs up for webinar → looks at a product page → clicks on a pay-per-click ad → attends a sales call → buys the product

In this marketing funnel example, if the business uses first-action attribution, then the lead and customer would be attributed to Twitter, because it was the first marketing event for the lead. This means that the revenue for this customer could be examined against the costs for Twitter to determine the ROI of not only social media, but Twitter-focused marketing efforts specifically.

In the method of last-action attribution, a lead and customer are attributed to the last marketing event prior to the sale. Looking at our marketing funnel example again, if this company uses last-action attribution, then the pay-per-click ad would be the attributed source of this lead and customer. See Figure 4.2 for a visual explanation of first versus last attribution.

Both first-action and last-action attribution have pros and cons. First-action attribution provides the intent and genesis of relationship with the lead, but it also ignores the key marketing tactic that drove the conversion. Although last-action attribution clearly identifies tactics that assist the visitor-to-lead conversion, it ignores how that visitor came to find your business in the first place. We tend to like first-action attribution better because it is a more accurate measure of initial intent and it is the cause of the prospect first raising his or her hand. In a perfect world, you

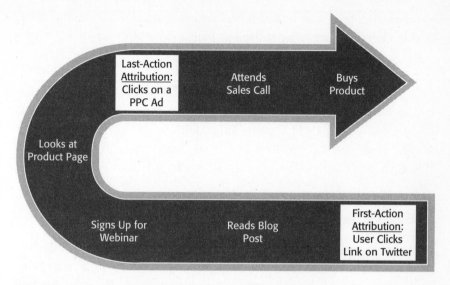

FIGURE 4.2   First Attribution versus Last Attribution

would measure both of these attribution models, as well as full lead to customer paths. Meaning we would look at all of the factors that cause a lead to become a customer. Many customers follow similar paths of content consumption before deciding to buy. However, to get started pick one of this methods and get going!

Gathering the Data

Deciding on an attribution method is only a part of building a plan to track B2B social media ROI. The second half is being able to collect data to use in B2B social media ROI calculations. When gathering the data, you need a tool or tools that can do the following tasks:

1. Segment website traffic by referral source
2. Set a cookie on a visitor's Web browser
3. Store lead and customer data

The devil is in the details, and the details in social media ROI is data collection. It doesn't need to be hard. Instead, it is about creating a closed-loop data gathering and reporting process for your business. Lead and customer data are normally stored in a customer relationship management (CRM) system, so it is critical to have a CRM system that is used by marketing and sales and that has an application programming interface (API) to talk to other software applications. Most major CRM systems, such as Salesforce.com, SugarCRM (SugarCRM.com), and NetSuite (NetSuite.com), have APIs and play well with other systems. For referral traffic and visitor tracking, you will need some combination of marketing automation and Web analytics software that can send and receive information with a CRM system. This could be a marketing automation system used with Google Analytics (Google.com/Analytics) or HubSpot (HubSpot.com), which combines both into one solution.

Measuring to Superstardom

Now that an attribution method is in place, along with tools for collecting data, it is time to understand the power unleashed by having access to this data. You waved this book in front of your supervisor's face and made him or her read this chapter to gain access to the data. Now use it! An easy mistake to make as a B2B marketer is to look at visits, leads, follows, or some other tactic-specific metric of success. The real metric for success and the one graph that will propel you faster than anything else into marketing superstardom is revenue generated by marketing activity.

And it is measured in dollars—or euros or yen or yuan.

It is this simple action of clearly measuring revenue by marketing activity that automatically elevates you into the top 1 percent of marketers. It is amazing how different a marketing team's performance looks when it is measured in dollars. Say goodbye to the doubting chief executive officer (CEO) who thinks marketing is only arts and crafts. Having this type of data helps you get a raise, a bonus, heck, even a new job.

Integrating Marketing and Sales Databases

To be a great company, the sales and marketing teams have to be in constant harmony. Seriously, this is important. If this currently isn't the case with your business, then find the best way to kiss and make up with the sales team. Although this applies to the management and team members of these two departments, it also applies to the systems used to run both teams. As marketers, measuring only visits and leads means you are ignoring the most important metric: revenue. Marketing's job is to support sales in driving customers, so it is critical to know which marketing efforts result in the most revenue. Salespeople should love you. You are helping them earn commissions. If they don't see it that way now, it is your job to change that perception.

When measuring ROI, a marketer must have the "R" and the "I." Integrating your Web analytics and leads database (marketing database) and CRM software (sales database) is the only way to clearly understand revenue by marketing channel. The path to marketing superstardom is paved with clear marketing-driven revenue charts. Traditionally, lead-to-customer conversion data are stored in a CRM system.

A marketer's favorite word should be *integration*. Success is based on the integration of people and tools. Being able to pass lead and Web analytics data from the marketing team into the sales database is critical in closing the loop on marketing-driven revenue. This means passing Web analytics data into a CRM and, ideally, having a Web analytics platform that tracks customers and that can pull customer data from a CRM system.

It Is Math, Not Hugs

Jay Baer, coauthor of *The Now Revolution*, summarized the myth of social media ROI perfectly on his blog.[1] According to Baer, saying "social media isn't measurable" is an excuse. Instead, what companies really mean when they say social media isn't measurable, is the following:

1. We don't have the right tools in place to collect the data we need.
2. When we have all the data, we don't know where to start.
3. We don't know which data might relate to other data to analyze it well.
4. We don't have or won't deploy enough data collection and analysis resources to figure this out.
5. We're afraid of what measuring will actually tell us about our effectiveness.

ROI is a clear number, derived from our simple formula: TLV − COCA/ COCA = ROI. Yes, marketing provides other value that is less quantifiable, such as brand awareness and word of mouth. However, qualitative metrics should always be secondary to ROI. ROI is your OxiClean. It makes everything cleaner, clearer, and impressive.

By understanding the ROI of not only the marketing team but also of individual marketing channels, you reach a level of marketing self-actualization. Decisions become much easier, because they are based in data. If your chief marketing officer (CMO) asked you the best way to spend an additional $50,000 of marketing investment, you would quickly know which channel would be best for the maximum return. This level of clear decision making and power automatically vaults you into the marketing elite.

Data is powerful, especially when you are talking about the right data. Getting caught up in number of fans, followers, and clicks is a quick way to demonstrate that you can't rise above the minutia of marketing tactics to see the bigger impact on the business. Don't be that kind of marketer. Be the one whom everyone admires because you have your thumb on the pulse of the business. Be agile enough to adjust marketing strategies to reflect current market conditions.

Marketing is an art and a science. This chapter took you through one of the most important parts of marketing science. Use the ROI formula, metrics, and ideas in this chapter to cement your place in marketing superstardom and to ward off any would-be pretenders who can't explain anything more than hugs—although you might want to give them a hug after you smack down their "increase in followers" report with a clean, clear demonstration of ROI.

Three B2B Social Media ROI Steps to Superstardom

1. *Determine COCA and TLV*—After reading about COCA and TLV, it is time to roll up your sleeves! Find an advocate on the management team who will aid in your requests to gather the financial data you need. Within 60 days of reading this chapter, you should plan on being able to determine TLV and COCA for your business.
2. *Decide on attribution*—You and your team need to decide on an attribution method for determining the ROI of your social media marketing efforts: first-action, last-action, or both. Schedule a one-hour meeting with relevant staff to discuss the pros and cons of each

method of attribution. Within a week following that meeting, have a final decision for the attribution model for your business and begin researching tools to aid in data collection and analysis.

3. *Integrate systems*—We are only on Chapter 4, and we have already asked you to do a lot. However, taking the time at the beginning of your social media marketing strategy to set up tools and integrate them will save countless hours in the future. In the first 90 days of your social media marketing efforts, implement and integrate analytics, marketing automation, and CRM systems to ensure that you can access and analyze sales and marketing data.

Reach

More Is Always Better

Reach is a fickle beast. It has become an almost taboo word for many business-to-business (B2B) marketers. Reach is one of those metrics that shows divergence between B2B and business-to-consumer (B2C) marketers. B2C marketers have long been obsessed with maximizing reach, whereas B2B marketers have zeroed in on targeting the best audience possible. Targeting is a key component of B2B marketing success, but not the only critical success factor.

Stop thinking of reach as a bad word! Realize that your B2C counterparts are onto something. To put it bluntly: B2B marketers should obsess over reach as much, if not more, than their B2C counterparts.

As marketers, it is easy to make premature or false assumptions about targeting and reach. The reality is that the best judge of targeting and quality leads is sales, not marketing. Conduct monthly surveys of the sales team to determine how their perception of lead quality changes along with shifts in marketing strategy.

Being Targeted Isn't Enough

Too many B2B marketers use "targeting the right prospects" as a scapegoat. In any B2B marketing conversation, it always seems to appear as the common objection. How many times have you been talking marketing with someone only to hear, "Yes, but are those (views, clicks, prospects, leads, etc.) targeted?" Let's end this irrational thinking once and for all.

Being targeted isn't enough in the age of the social web.

Think back to what we learned in Chapter 3 about search engines elevating social signals such as likes, comments, tweets, and shares to determine how a website ranks for a keyword. Let's translate this to reach. Search engines reward companies that have more reach with increased organic search traffic. Because of this, focusing on targeting and dwindling down your reach becomes a detriment.

The argument for being targeted is often the argument against B2B social media adoption within a company. The argument often goes something like this, "We only have 10 possible customers, why should we waste time with social media?" This way of thinking completely ignores influencers. Yes, a business may only have 10 prospective customers, but those 10 companies may contain multiple decision makers who are influenced by a chain of hundreds, if not thousands, of people. Ignoring reach in B2B marketing is a classic example of allowing the status quo to take over and preach ideas that sound good but aren't the best for your business.

Be Able to Sell Anything

None of us is Nostradamus. It is impossible to predict the future of a business or an industry. Because of this simple fact, we as marketers must be prepared to *be able to sell anything*. Many great innovations have been happy accidents. 3M hit the jackpot with Post-it Notes when a scientist was working on an adhesive for a completely different project and by accident created a revolutionary product. If a happy accident like this were to happen to your business, would your marketing team be ready? If your marketing is only targeted, it loses sight of possible shifts in product development and business strategy.

What if your business changed tomorrow? Start-ups call this pivoting, and they do it all the time. Does your marketing team have the talent, reach, and expertise to adjust? It is important to focus on building reach that is both directly and tangentially targeted to your ideal buyer personas.

Five Questions for Better Reach Building

1. Who influences my target audience?
2. Whom does my target audience influence?
3. Who is most influential online in my industry?
4. What industries are related to my target industry?
5. What jobs do the people below and above my targeted personas traditionally have in a business hierarchy?

These five questions should help uncover new audiences related to your target audience that should be considered for marketing and reach-building efforts.

Six Time-Tested Methods for Building Reach

The desire to build reach isn't a new obsession for marketers. Reach has long been the focus of B2C marketers. Reach is about building the tip-top of the marketing funnel. Reach building is about driving more traffic to a business website, increasing e-mail opt-ins, and adding new social media followers. Take some cues from the B2C folks and apply some of their time-tested strategies for reach building to your next B2B social media campaign.

1. *Launch a contest*—When looking to fill the top of the marketing funnel, it is important to cast a wide net. One way to do this is to host a contest. The key to a great contest is to minimize the friction for the person to enter. Contests that involve a lot of work, such as submitting a video or filling out a long form, often fall short of their goal. Instead, focus on offering a compelling prize that is in some way tied to your business. Require only an e-mail address or a share on Twitter. Sometimes, if the prize is compelling enough, it is possible to ask for more than these low-friction entry points.

2. *Ask for the connection*—Too many B2B marketers make assumptions that prospects can read their minds. Instead, it is important to ask prospects clearly and directly to take the action you want. In the case of reach building, it is asking them to take actions like signing up for an e-mail list or following your company on social media. Look at existing e-mails, print materials, and trade show booths, and think about how they can be adapted to ask your audience to connect.

3. *Build links*—Getting more inbound links to your website is important for building reach in two ways. First, it helps your company website rank higher in search results, which provides more free search traffic. Second, it means more referral traffic from other websites. Refer to Chapter 3 for some techniques to build more links to your website.

4. *Make opting in and following easy*—Friction is the enemy of the marketing superstar. Friction is what stops people from taking the action you want them to take. Friction kills conversion rates and is one of the reasons your e-mail list, blog subscribers, and social media connections aren't at the level you would like. One of the fastest ways to build reach is to reduce friction. This is done by making it easy for website visitors to follow you on social media. Many popular platforms such as

Twitter and Facebook provide buttons that allow a website visitor to follow or like your company with one click. Remember: fewer clicks, less friction.

5. *Beef up content creation*—Building reach is partly a matter of probability. Remarkable content is key, but so is having a lot of it. The more content that you create, the higher the likelihood that your company will be found by prospects. One of the best ways to create more content to be found is to have a business blog. Read the blogging chapter of this book for everything you need to know to be a blogging expert.

6. *Tell a story*—It is not about you. It is about your customers and the problems they are trying to solve. It may sound simple, but being able to tell an interesting story that addresses prospects' key concerns is one of the best reach-building tools out there. The Web allows publishing and interaction to happen easier now than ever before. This means that each day it gets harder to earn the attention of your target audience. Having a story helps you stand out from the competition and get attention when everyone else is being ignored.

Remarkable and Frequent Content Fuels Reach

Getting found on the Web is a lot like winning the lottery. A person who has 100 tickets has a much better chance of winning the lottery than a person with only 1 ticket. In the world of social media, content is the equivalent of lottery tickets. Data from HubSpot's 2011 State of Inbound Marketing Report[1] shows that companies with more indexed pages on their website generate more leads on a monthly basis. As seen in Figure 5.1, companies with fewer than 60 pages on their website generate only 5 leads per month on average, whereas companies with 311 pages or more on their website generate, on average, 75 leads per month.

Content creation is the underbelly of the beast that is social media. The marketers who don't make it to superstardom get distracted by bright and shiny tools. Great and frequent content creation makes up for lack of mastery of social media tools. To be a marketing superstar, you don't have to spend every waking minute discovering and learning the latest and greatest social media tools. Instead, you simply need to be the best brand journalist in your industry. Half of being great at social media marketing is knowing how to tell a great story on the Web; the other half is having the discipline

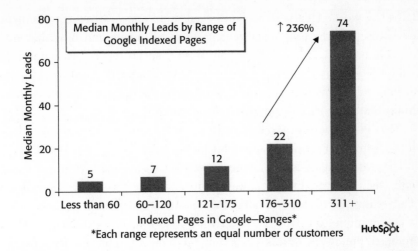

FIGURE 5.1 Average Leads per Month for Number of Website Pages

and the resolve to create content day after day, week after week, and month after month.

No marketing superstar is built overnight; it only seems that way. Ask any marketer you idealize how he or she achieved his or her career position and what will follow will be a story that isn't glamorous, but instead calculated and filled with hard work. The biggest secret in B2B social media marketing is that those companies that create great content consistently over time are the ones that succeed. Look at our own site SocialMediaB2B.com. We started it in February 2009, but it was months before we had any real readership. In the early months, it is easy to conceive of giving up. Some of our best early posts hardly gained any traction at all. But they helped us set the tone and the operating rhythm for the site.

Don't give up. Trust that you are on the path of marketing truth and justice. It doesn't matter that nobody has read your first blog post. It matters how many people read your 20th and 100th blog posts—and that you write those posts.

Paying for Reach Is Okay

A lot of what makes social media appealing as a marketing and reach-building strategy is its ability to drive impressive results with very little hard costs. Well, that is aside from the time of salaried staff or contractors doing the work. This cost becomes even more appealing as management teams discover the long-term benefits of social media and how they differ from paid advertising. Although organic social media reach building is important, it is also important to understand that buying social media reach is okay. This section will be mocked by the social media purist who thinks that hugging customers fixes everything.

Don't get us wrong. We love our customers, but we need them to buy things from us or we don't stay in business.

The reason paying for social media reach can be a good investment, especially when compared with traditional media, is that it has all the immediacy of advertising combined with all of the long-term benefits of social media.

For example, on Twitter's advertising platform, one product is called Promoted Followers. In this advertising product, your business pays Twitter in an auction format for new followers. Twitter displays your account to users who share interests that you have targeted in your account. Every time a user follows your account from these paid placements, you pay Twitter a fee. The fee is set on a bidding system.

What makes paying for social media reach different from a trade magazine ad is the potential value that can be driven by a paid follower. That paid follower could become a lead, share your content with other prospects, or even recommend you to others who will follow you. This expands your reach. This follower doesn't go away as soon as you stop paying Twitter. Sure, he or she can choose to unfollow you, but as long as you are engaging and providing relevant content, that's not likely to happen.

Twitter isn't the only social media platform that offers these types of advertising opportunities. LinkedIn and Facebook offer very similar products, and it is likely that other social networks will adopt this revenue generation model in the future.

Paying for reach, however, is worthwhile only if you have done the math to determine the value of a follower on a given social network. Look at your organic cost per lead for a social media channel such as Twitter and determine how many paid followers it would take to drive one lead for your business.

Let's say that you get 10 leads per month from Twitter and that your company has 1,000 Twitter followers. That means for every 100 followers, on average, your company gets one lead. So, at 50 cents per follower, 100 followers would cost $50. If your target cost per lead is *less* than $50, then paying for followers is not going to be the best investment for your business. However, if your cost per lead is high, something like $250, because you sell big-ticket items, then paying $50 for a lead is a great deal.

Look at the math. Determine whether paying for social media reach is right for your business. If it is, it is a better investment than some of your current paid media commitments.

Nearsightedness Kills Great Marketing

Don't be nearsighted. Think for scale and for the long term. One of the fastest ways to fall from marketing superstardom is to fall victim to nearsightedness. Sacrificing reach for the sake of being targeted is often one of the first symptoms of marketing nearsightedness. For you as a marketer, being nearsighted means thinking about the results and needs of the company today only, or even this month.

Marketing superstars see the big picture. They are active participants in their companies. They break out of their comfort zones and interact with team members from other departments. It is this activity within the company that helps great marketers understand the vision and the direction of the company. This knowledge is priceless. Understanding the direction your company will be taking in the next 6 months, 12 months, or even longer empowers you not only to build reach in these new areas but to create content and all the important aspects of marketing that can help propel new products, services, partnerships, and more.

Put on your glasses. Don't limit your strategy and vision to the short term. Build reach that is relevant for the state of your business not only today, but also in the future.

Three B2B Social Media Reach Building Steps to Superstardom

1. *Build tangential reach*—When looking to expand your marketing strategy, focus on your core audience as well as adjacent audiences. Answer the *Five Questions for Better Reach Building* from this chapter. Identify two buyer personas that are related to your core persona and begin actively targeting them in your reach-building efforts.
2. *Increase overall reach*—Take a cue from B2C companies and implement as many of the *Six Time-Tested Methods for Building Reach* as

possible. Before you begin to test these methods, document your overall marketing reach (e-mail list, social media followers, blog subscribers, etc.), as well as your marketing reach by channel. Over time, look at the correlation between your reach growth and the growth of new leads generated.

3. *Set a content consistency plan*—For a 90-day period, create a calendar for how frequently you will commit to creating content. Set a frequency for each type of content. The minimum should be at least one blog post per week, at least one webinar in the 90-day period, and at least one social media message per day. Following this 90-day commitment, look at your Web analytics and CRM systems to determine the impact of these efforts for building reach and generating leads.

Social Media Lead Generation in Action

Creating Ebooks and Webinars That Prospects Love

Social media and landing pages are only part of your lead generation machine. The hidden hero in the social media lead generation, or lead generation in general for that matter, is the offer. An offer is a piece of content or service extended by a company in exchange for personal information. In short, the offer is the catalyst. You can have the best landing page on Earth, but with a poor offer, it is worthless. A great lead generation offer is one of the most important tools in your marketing tool belt. Think Batman's grappling hook. A great offer can help you reach what may seem like unreasonable lead generation goals or turn a plain-Jane landing page into a lead generation machine.

When thinking about offers, you should place them into two distinct buckets. The first bucket is for top of the funnel (TOFU) offers. The second is for middle of the funnel (MOFU) offers. TOFU offers are traditionally content-focused offers such as ebooks, white papers, and webinars that address broad problems for prospects and provide industry insight. MOFU offers are more product-centric and help move buyers further through the buying cycle. These offers can be free consultations, product demonstrations, free product trials, and other content or services closely related to the product or services being sold. Think of TOFU offers like a fun phone call for a second date, whereas MOFU offers are more like a freshly made key being presented right before the question, "Will you move in with me?"

Sample Scenario

A manufacturer of hospital beds is looking to drive more hospital administrators as leads. An effective TOFU offer could be a free ebook titled: *10 Best Practices for Improving Hospital Facilities Management.* An effective MOFU offer could be a free 30-minute phone consultation to determine opportunities for cost savings.

Every marketing superstar needs both TOFU and MOFU offers to help move prospects through a long, competitor-laden and budget-restricted business-to-business (B2B) buying cycle. Since MOFU offers are often very specific and unique to each company or industry, this chapter will predominately focus on creating awe-inspiring TOFU offers that will leave your prospects begging for more.

Create Ebooks Everyone Wants

Ebooks. White papers. What's the difference? The ebook is the white paper's more modern cousin. Both are written pieces of content that can be anywhere from 10 to 50 pages in length. They are more in-depth than a blog post, but briefer than a book. Traditionally, white papers have been more academic in tone and style. Although an ebook may strive to educate on the same topic, it would do so in a more entertaining tone, accompanied by images to help illustrate its points. Both ebooks and white papers have their place in your vault of awesome offers depending on your audience. Go for the ebook instead of the white paper when talking to nontechnical audiences.

What's that? Why? Don't smack us for putting ebooks ahead of white papers on our list of awesome lead generation offers. Ebooks win for one simple reason: infotainment. In the world of cell phones, laptops, tablets, and seemingly endless distractions, being informative isn't enough. Marketers today also have to entertain while informing, hence infotainment. B2B isn't a synonym for boring. The marketers who win in the coming years will be those who understand that infotainment-based content stands out. Stop producing boring brochures and product pages! Get creative and leverage ebooks as a tool to show your company's knowledge and expertise.

All content has a formula for success. Ebooks are no different than anything else. Before your ebook is ready to be downloaded by eager prospects, it has to be content they need. Think for a second why you fill out a form online. Simple. You are looking for an answer to a problem. A great ebook first and foremost solves a common problem that your leads encounter related to your business. Not sure what a few might be? Dive into your e-mail inbox and take a look at the questions you or the sales team have answered recently. See a theme? Those common and repetitive questions are most often the genesis of great ebooks. The clear and applicable idea is the most important part, but then comes the writing and layout. Don't worry; we have you covered.

The 10-Step Blueprint to Ebook Awesomeness

1. *Eye-grabbing title*—With everything your target buyers have on their plates, they need to be enticed not just to download your ebook but to actually carve out some time to read it. Your title should be concise and actionable. Some examples of effective ebook title formulas are:
   - [Insert Number] of Ways to [Insert Problem That the Lead Is Trying to Solve]
   - The Essential Guide to [Insert Problem That the Lead Is Trying to Solve]
   - [Insert Number] of Ways to Do More [Insert Problem That the Lead Is Trying to Solve] with Less
   - [Insert Number] Mistakes Not to Make on [Insert Problem That the Lead Is Trying to Solve]
   - A Step-by-Step Guide to [Insert Problem That the Lead Is Trying to Solve]
2. *Ebook template*—All of your ebooks should follow the same style. This reinforces branding and helps ensure that you don't forget any important components to a successful ebook. The template doesn't need to be created in a long design process. A nice-looking template could even be done in Microsoft Word or PowerPoint. But please don't use those default design templates or clip art. Consistency helps set the right expectations with your leads, and a template is the key method for ensuring consistency.

3. *Frequent headers*—Once your brilliant title has your leads setting aside time to read your ebook, the next step is to transform them into engaged readers who hang on every word you write. Do this by using headers to break up long sections of text. This use of headers makes your content easier to read and provides opportunities for you to write mini-headlines that keep a reader engaged. How many headers is enough? Zoom out to Print Preview of your document and slowly scroll. Do you feel overwhelmed at any point by a page that has long sections of text without headers? If this is the case, then it is likely the document could use a few more.

4. *Pictures*—Online or offline, pictures set expectations and pull us into a piece of content. Pictures are also a key differentiator between ebooks and white papers. The same rules with headers apply to pictures. They make things more engaging and make them easier to read. A good rule of thumb is to include a picture at least once in every two pages of an ebook.

5. *Emphasis boxes*—Were you a journalist in a former life or a frequent magazine reader? If so, you are likely familiar with pull quotes. This is the practice of taking an important statement given to a reporter and enlarging it and setting it in a prominent location on the page. As an ebook writer and editor, take a cue from the publishing world and create emphasis boxes that contain critical data or statements. Give these boxes a different design element such as a gray or light-colored background instead of white to draw the reader's attention to the information that you most want them to remember.

6. *Links to related content*—Remember that the "e" in ebooks is for "electronic" and many of your leads will be reading the ebook on an electronic device. Because of this, it is important to include links to credible third-party sources, as well as relevant content on your company website.

7. *The right file name*—Good content gets shared. By following the steps in this blueprint, you are well on your way to creating a compelling ebook. It is likely that your leads will e-mail the ebook file to their coworkers for their thoughts. Because of this, you always want to include the name of your company in the file name of the download so that other readers will associate the valuable content with your company. The file name should be executed in this

style: [Name of Ebook] [Company Name].pdf. It is bad form, and kind of lame, to include extra words like final or revision in the file name.

8. *Social sharing links*—Current leads are a great referral source. Make it easy for them to tell others about the great content you create. Include social sharing buttons at the bottom of each ebook page that will quickly and easily allow them to share the landing page for the ebook on social networks such as LinkedIn and Facebook.

9. *Clear takeaways*—Conclusions are passive. Prime your leads for action. Instead of ending your ebook with a conclusion, try summarizing important action items at the end and encourage readers to begin to take these actions for their businesses.

10. *Call to action*—Yes, if a person has already downloaded your ebook, then he or she is a lead. That isn't enough. Use ebooks as a way to progress leads through the buying cycle. At the end of the ebook, include a CTA for a MOFU offer that will move leads closer to purchasing. Ebooks are lead generation gold. Use them to educate leads and establish credibility in your industry.

Webinars Are Low-Cost Trade Shows

A key lead generation source for many B2B companies are trade shows. There are many ways to enhance the trade show experience with social media, but that is another chapter. Instead, let's talk about saving some marketing budget by reducing those expensive trade shows and replacing them with webinars. Webinars are online presentations that involve a pre-registered audience joining the same audio line and signing into a service on their computer to watch slides accompanied by the speaker's voice.

Nothing can replace the person-to-person communications of a trade show; however, webinars can attract an engaged and targeted audience that does not have the time or money to attend an industry trade show. Unlike trade shows, webinars can also be recorded for on-demand viewing, making them even more convenient. A webinar is typically led by an expert within your company or a noncompetitive third party and lasts somewhere between 30 and 60 minutes.

Instead of sending a five-figure invoice to finance for a trade show, webinars can be conducted for relatively low costs. Tools like GoToWebinar and WebEx allow you to hold unlimited attendance webinars for a monthly fee of less than $100. On the cost and convenience scorecards, webinars win. The mechanics for generating leads from webinars are very similar to that of ebooks. Establish a date for the webinar, create a landing page, and once a person has completed the form, he or she is sent the log-in information.

The key to a great webinar is to remember that the personal connection that speakers and attendees love about trade shows doesn't exist in the same way. During webinars, speakers are also competing with distractions such as the attendee's e-mail inbox and current projects. These factors make presenting and producing a webinar different than presenting in person.

Five Steps for an Engaging Webinar

1. *Have an in-person audience*—Even if it is only one person, have someone else in the room with you while presenting a webinar. As speakers, we all use feedback from the audience to adjust our presentation. Since you can't see the people listening to you on a webinar, having a coworker sit in as an audience to provide feedback is invaluable.

2. *Use more slides*—Since listeners are at their computers and easily distracted, use many highly visual slides. Instead of cramming five bullet points on one slide, make each point its own slide and add an image relevant to that point. Having more slides allows you to update the visuals more often to retain the attention of your audience.

3. *Call attention to slides*—If a webinar attendee has fallen off the wagon and is checking his or her inbox, you need to bring that person back to the presentation. Use verbal cues such as, "Look at this" or "I love this chart" to call everyone's attention back to your presentation.

4. *E-mail the video and slides*—If people are too busy taking notes, you don't really have their attention. Before the webinar starts, inform the audience that they will be e-mailed a link to the video of the webinar recording and a copy of the slides. This will put the audience at rest and allow them to focus on the presenter instead of their notepad.

5. *Provide shareable takeaways*—In the midst of your infotainment, use slides to provide a brief simple sentence takeaway or lesson about the information that was most recently presented. These takeaways will be shared on social media or be the few notes taken that will be shared with other members of the listener's team. Either way, it enables the presenter of the webinar to dictate the key pieces of information in the presentation.

Webinars rock. Use them to move social media dialog to a more personal form of content that captures the attention and mind of your leads.

Marketing with Existing Sales Tools

Ann Handley, coauthor of the book *Content Rules,* has many rules for creating great content and offers. However, her favorite rule is also one of our favorites: Don't recycle; reimagine your content. The fact of the matter is, when it comes to creating marketing offers that rock, you have already done most of the work.

Between sales collateral, company reports, industry research, and all the other work that has been done by marketing, a wealth of information exists to be reimagined. This chapter has covered many best practices for creating and producing great ebooks and webinars, but the truth is that you know your target persona better than anyone else. You also know what information about your industry and your company best resonates with prospects. Take a minute and make a few notes about what information should be a key part of your B2B social media marketing plan.

Once you have a clear handle on key content pieces and ideas, it is time to conduct a content audit. Go through your computer's hard drive or the company server and take inventory of what content you currently have. Now, with a clearer idea on what is available, set priorities for turning some of it into your next ebook or webinar.

Storytelling with Video

Video is more important for B2B companies than their business-to-consumer (B2C) counterparts. Sure B2C companies have their 30-second spots, but B2B companies have complex products that can be simplified immensely with video. Video is key to all B2B social media content, even going beyond offers to blog posts and other areas of communication.

Web video is different from all other formats of video. Video on the Internet must be short, clear, funny, emotional, and well produced. To be clear, well produced doesn't mean a Hollywood studio shoot. Instead, it means a well-thought-out concept and production values that merit the idea that is trying to be communicated. For example, if you are working on a customer case study video, instead of a 10-minute video of the customer talking, cut it down to three minutes with video clips of the customer, video clips of your product or service in action, charts and data, results, and so forth. These other shots are called B-roll and help make the video more interesting to watch. Local news stories do a great job of breaking up talking head videos with B-roll. Thinking about how to build an interesting video before you shoot it is the vast majority of quality production value.

Three Commandments of B2B Video

1. *Always go shorter*—Don't get caught making excuses why a video needs to be longer. It doesn't. In fact, it needs to be shorter. Perfection in B2B video is not when there is nothing left to add in, but instead when there is nothing left to remove. Use three minutes as your watermark. Never let a video exceed three minutes and strive for ways to make it shorter. The Web moves fast, and three minutes is an eternity on the Web.
2. *Be entertaining*—B2B companies are fun, too. Prospective customers want to be informed and entertained. Add elements of humor and emotion into your video. Take some time to storyboard the video ahead of time to ensure you are telling a story, not simply making a video. Some of the best B2B videos, such as Blendtec's "Will It Blend" (WillItBlend.com) series and Grasshopper's "New Dork,"[1] have used humor and entertainment to the tune of infotaining millions of people.
3. *Cast correctly*—Like a movie, you must pick the right actors to tell your story. Some employees are great on camera, whereas others aren't. Don't pick the most knowledgeable person for a B2B video; instead pick the person that is best in front of a camera.

LESSONS FROM A MARKETING SUPERSTAR

Name: Lisa A. Burns
Title: Manager, Corporate Communications
Company: Corning Incorporated
Years in Position: 6
What is your greatest social media/marketing success?
That would be Corning's "A Day Made of Glass" viral video. The video has received over 15 million views on YouTube since

launching it in February 2011, with 8 million of those views just a month after it was first posted. The video strikes a balance between an understanding of materials technology and people's imagination for what their future holds—and succeeded in portraying a world people want to share with others. In that first month, most discussion of the video was spread between blogs (57 percent of mentions), online forums (23 percent), and Twitter (11 percent), with the traditional news media at just 9 percent of total mentions.

What is your biggest roadblock in executing your social media strategy? It is clear that just having a social media presence is not enough to be successful. Making the ongoing commitment and investment in rich, innovative content that target audiences value is critical for success. That steady content stream can be a challenge to maintain.

What is the single most important trait of a B2B marketer? Someone who truly understands the target audience and then designs a strategy and related marketing program that will be valued by that audience.

To YouTube or Not to YouTube, That Is the Question

When the topic of video comes up, one of the inevitable questions is about maximizing search engine optimization benefits from video and how YouTube fits into the puzzle. YouTube, the Web's largest video-sharing service, is the second largest search engine on the Internet. For B2B companies looking to use video to build reach for their business, YouTube is a must. However, it isn't always best for maximizing search engine optimization benefits. Although you should upload a video to YouTube, you should also create a video site map for your website or blog.

A video site map is something your information technology (IT) team or website management vendor can help you with. Google provides in-depth information on their Webmaster forum on how to create a video site map.[2] Essentially a video site map is some code that helps explain to

Google that you have a video on your website and what the content of that video is. Giving Google this information is clearly valuable for improving search engine optimization and providing Google with ranking information.

However, this doesn't mean that YouTube is worthless from a search engine optimization standpoint. As we talked about in Chapter 3 search engines are using social signals to rank websites, so the reach and shares that can be generated by uploading a video to YouTube are important. In addition, YouTube reserves the first 30 characters of each video description for a link. This means that before writing a description for your video, you should enter a target link on your website in an effort to create another inbound link to that page. Again, referring back to the search chapter, inbound links are another important factor in your website being discovered through search engine.

Being Interesting Is the New Black

All of the insights and tips provided in the chapter fail in the absence of a great story. Social media has made it easy for marketers to become publishers, meaning the Web is now full of product-centric, boring content. The path to marketing superstardom is lined with the ability to tell a great story in any type of media. Offers like ebooks and webinars provide an opportunity to tell a richer and more complete story. Use the capability for richness to your advantage, instead of stacking up more company-centric, not buyer-centric, information.

Black is always in style, and so is telling a great story.

Three B2B Social Media Content Offer Steps to Superstardom

1. *Become a title-writing machine*—Titles are core to the success of generating leads with ebooks, webinars, and other types of offers. Test the five different headline formulas provided in the ebook blueprint section by writing a blog post using each headline. Look at the performance of the blog posts in terms of visits and leads to pick a winning formula. Use that same formula to write an ebook on the same topic within 90 days of completing the headline test.

2. *Experiment with webinars*—Look at your trade show budget and determine how many leads you would need to generate with webinars to justify a reduction in budget. Conduct a series of webinars over the next quarter to accurately determine their lead generation potential for your business. If that number meets or exceeds your required projections, then reduce trade show budgets in favor of webinars and report the reduction in cost per lead to the management team.

3. *Check for storytelling*—Stop creating content people don't want. Before you publish an ebook or schedule a webinar, ask yourself one important question: "Would I read or watch this?" If it isn't worth your time, then it isn't worth your prospects' time. In addition to asking yourself that important question, conduct a survey of your prospects to determine what topics and pieces of content they would most like to see from your company.

Why You Are Already a Business Blogging Expert

Whether you are a new marketer or an old hand at crafting your company's message and disseminating it, you already possess the skills to run a successful blog. As you follow along on the path to marketing superstardom, you will find that a tweak to your skills is all that's needed to get your company blog up and running.

It's okay if you don't have a blog yet. Wait. You are not going to create one? Close the book now. We are done.

We can't help you generate leads and connect with your prospects if you are not able to create a blog on your company website. A blog is the hub of your company's business-to-business (B2B) social media presence as seen in Figure 7.1. All inbound traffic from social media postings should drive to your blog. A blog allows your business to quickly publish content in a search engine–friendly manner to spark social media discussion.

It shows how the people of your company think, as well as the values of the business. Prospects like that. Your business blog is regularly updated with keyword-driven content. Search engines like that. It can answer questions about the company's products and services. Prospects like that. As people click on links to get the answers to their questions, traffic to the posts increases. Search engines like that. Valuable and entertaining content makes readers want to share posts with their social networks. Everyone likes that.

Social media sharing impacts search results, as we saw in Chapter 3, at both the search level, by factoring in people's social connections, and at the search results level, by including pages, or in this case blog posts, shared by social connections.

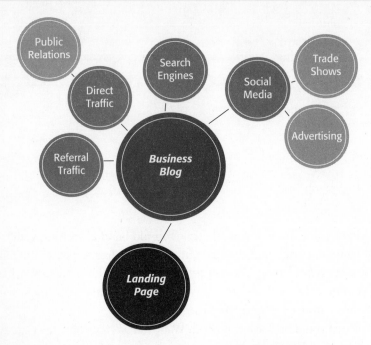

FIGURE 7.1 The Blog as a Hub of Social Media Leads

The Origins of Corporate Blogging

Technically oriented people started creating and updating blogs, online journals originally called weblogs, in the 1990s. Blogger was the first software interface, developed in 1999, that made publishing to the Web easy for anyone who wasn't a programmer. The first companies to start blogging were technology companies, such as Microsoft, Google, Sun Microsystems, and Cisco. They understood blogging as a new medium to communicate with customers in a different way. This was the beginning of the conversation.

Conversation has two meanings in this case. The first refers to two-way communication enabled by blog comments. The second refers to the sometimes conversational tone of the content shared on corporate blogs. Even in the beginning, companies understood that a blog was not just another place to publish a press release.

In 1994, then–Microsoft technical evangelist Robert Scoble, wrote the following on his personal blog, as the first of several reasons why companies should blog. *"People don't trust corporations. Especially big and successful ones like, um, Microsoft. Come on, be honest, none of you really trust us to* do the right thing, do you? So, how do we show you that we're trustworthy? We need to invite you deep inside our corporate structures and talk to you like human beings. It's exactly why Channel 9 [a Microsoft video blog] resonates with so many of you."[1]

Traditionally, B2B companies have produced content to generate leads. Those case studies and white papers lived behind a gate on a corporate website, and they were not easy to promote or share. The ideas in them certainly did not spread. Now social media gives your company a platform to speak from, and the use of social media increases the reach of the message. This content, when deployed thoughtfully on a blog, can be used to drive leads for your company.

The Thinking Part of Setting Up Your Business Blog

Social media marketing does not happen in a silo. It needs to connect to your company's business goals. Companies may want to increase sales, reduce costs or improve customer satisfaction, and social media can help with those by generating leads and providing a more efficient customer service channel. These goals determine everything about your company's approach to blogging, from what it looks like to the topics covered.

Once you determine your goals, create a list of strategies to reach these goals. These strategies help determine the functional look and feel of your blog. For example, if a blog needs to generate leads, one strategy is to include calls to action at the end of blog posts. If providing customer support is a function of a blog, share as much information as possible on the blog to reduce incoming calls and e-mails for support. And if your blog is about demonstrating thought leadership or becoming an industry leading resource, determine strategies that relate to those.

Many B2B companies have developed personas of their marketing targets. Those personas are the readers of your blog. This means understanding your customers' concerns and information consumption habits. If a blog is directed at a busy chief information officer (CIO) who is more likely to search the Internet on a mobile device, this influences not just what a blog looks like, but what kinds of articles are included and how they are written. Conversely, if a purchasing agent is one of the personas targeted, the blog would have a very different style and tone.

If you have run any Google search ads, you have a list of keywords. We talked about keywords and search in Chapter 3. Use your unified keyword strategy as a starting point for your blog content. Your business blog could ultimately be the biggest source of search engine traffic for your website. Google provides a keyword search tool that gives marketers a list of highly searched terms based on particular words and phrases, or even a website address. If you install Google Analytics or Google Webmaster Tools on your company website, you can see the keywords that currently drive traffic to your website.

The most important part of a Web page, from a search perspective, is the page title. In most cases with a blog, that is also the blog post title. These titles should use keywords that prospects are searching for. These keywords are also important for discovery when blog posts are shared on social media profiles. These keywords should be naturally included in the first paragraph or two of the post as well.

In most marketing copy, a product is called by its proper name or certain approved general terms. Blog posts are great places to use alternative keywords that describe the product to drive additional search traffic. This sometimes makes marketers crazy, because even though these alternate descriptions have high search volume, they may not follow company usage standards. "We can't write about conveyor belts because our systems don't use belts. I don't care what people are looking for." You need to understand what your customers and prospects call your products. Examine the search volume for different keyword options and make smart choices that will impact the business's goals.

Cybersecurity company BreakingPoint (www.breakingpointsystems.com/community/blog/) not only has created blog categories from their keywords, but has integrated the blog content with similar keyword-based content on their website in one menu as seen in Figure 7.2.

The Content Part of Setting Up Your Blog

A business blog needs content, and the most common question from marketers is: What should I write about? The first step in answering that question is to develop a content strategy. A content strategy can be considered the marketing plan for a blog. It is based on the target audience, or personas, and breaks down the categories of posts by those audiences.

FIGURE 7.2   Blog Categories Are Integrated in BreakingPoint Systems' Website Navigation

It doesn't just include the topics of the posts, but also includes the types of posts to publish. A content strategy for a blog that is developed to drive leads also includes the kinds of calls to action on the various types of posts.

Make the content strategy real by developing an editorial calendar. Marketing superstars are prized for their organization and their planning skills. Nobody should ever sit down and say: "It's Wednesday, and I need to write a blog post. What should I write about?" Create an editorial calendar for a month at a time. Depending on your approval process, work at least one to two weeks ahead of schedule. Even if no approval process is needed, the editorial calendar will guide the process.

The next question marketers ask is how often they should publish blog posts. This depends on how many people will contribute to the blog, but the goal should be one to three times per week. More blog posts drive more traffic and leads, so find a frequency that you can maintain, as consistency is also important. A spreadsheet is the perfect tool to organize the editorial calendar.

One of the biggest challenges in managing a blog for a large company is wrangling other company employees to post to the blog as well. If you try to publish a blog without help, you may not be able to publish frequently enough. And unless you take on the role of a brand journalist, you will be unable to tell stories that broadly represent the company. The Indium Corporation (Indium.com), makers of electrically conductive solder paste, has 12 engineers and the director of marketing communications blogging regularly.

Start by looking at each functional area and see if anyone is already blogging or active on social media. These are the most likely candidates. Food bloggers do count, because they already understand the medium. If someone is already blogging about your industry on his or her own blog, consider excerpting those blog posts on the company blog.

Training company bloggers is about much more than showing people how to use blogging software. That is the smallest part of training, if needed at all. Writing blog posts in e-mails or Word documents is a totally acceptable workflow, as long as you and the marketing team have the time to convert these to blog posts.

New company bloggers need to be trained to think like bloggers. They need to learn what makes a good blog post and how it should be written. How-to articles make great blog posts, for example "Four ways Indiana Jones would reorganize your warehouse" or "Six ways your printer can prepare you for space travel."

New bloggers need a blog ideas file in one place. Whether it is a small notebook or a note file on their smartphone, it needs to be something that is always with them. Suggest that they come up with three or four times the number of ideas that they need. For example, if they are posting once per month, they should have three or four ideas to choose from each month.

Share success stories of customers and prospects engaging on the blog or sales that have closed as a result of the blog. This will highlight for employees the value of blogging and motivate them to keep contributing regular posts.

The Nuts and Bolts Part of Setting Up Your Blog

A blog should be hosted on your company's domain. This means its address is blog.company.com or company.com/blog. There is no reason for a company blog to be hosted on WordPress.com or Google's blog platform (blogger .com). One of the things your company blog does is attract search traffic to blog posts. If the blog is hosted elsewhere, a strong blog presence drives traffic to

WordPress and Google. And *they* don't need traffic; your company website does. Another advantage of hosting your blog on the company domain is that Google Analytics or other Web analytics program is fully integrated and can show how traffic moves from blog content to website content.

Author photos show the people of a company beyond a voice on the telephone or the words in an e-mail. Another benefit of author photos is that they link to a writer's online presence and personal brand. Authors should use the same photo on the blog that they use on Twitter and LinkedIn, making it easy for customers and prospects to recognize them across multiple social platforms. This can be a good way to encourage writers to use their official company photo on their social profile.

When you spend time creating and maintaining a blog, the last thing you should do is hide it. Don't play hide and seek with your efforts. Yes, people will arrive at single blog posts through both search and social media links, but make sure visitors to your company website can find it too. Some successful ways to direct visitors to a blog include listing it in the main navigation of the site, featuring a feed of the most recent articles on the home page and showing a visit our blog button in the sidebar throughout all pages of the website.

GE Global Research (ge.geglobalresearch.com) does all three of these and two of them are seen in Figure 7.3. The blog is listed in the main navigation,

FIGURE 7.3 GE Research Website Displays Blog Links in Two Places

there is a feed of the most recent post on the home page, and there is a feed of recent posts by relevant category in the sidebar of Web content pages.

The Ultimate Business Blogging Checklist

Business blogging is a core component of successful social media lead generation. Follow this checklist to ensure your content creation efforts will be rewarded.

1. *Create compelling written content*—Is this sentence compelling? Does it make you want to do something? How about this one? In our case it needs to make you keep reading. On a blog the first step is determining what *compelling content* even means. It doesn't just mean interesting and valuable to the audience, but interesting and valuable in such a way that it compels them to take action. This starts with a headline that makes people click on a search result, a Twitter link, or even a Facebook update. That click is the first step of drawing prospects into the funnel. Once they arrive at the post, or other Web content, they will likely consume it. Don't think about food bloggers here. In the case of written content, *consume* means they will read it, or in the case of many Web surfers who are grazing, they will skim it. Does anyone even call it *Web surfing* anymore?

   Now the next step is for them to take another action. That could be to share it with their social networks, e-mail it to their work colleagues, leave a comment, or click on the call-to-action (CTA) link at the end of the blog post.

   What? No CTAs on blog posts?

   Remember, this is B2B marketing, and we are trying to drive leads.

   The content brings people to the top of the funnel, and when it is compelling enough, people enter the funnel with that next click. Think of a blog post as a primer on a topic. It helps provide a basic understanding of an idea, but to get more information, a blog reader needs to download a related ebook. A link to the ebook should be included at the end of a blog post to maximize the number of visitors who read your posts and then become leads for your sales team.

   The best place to start when creating great written content is to start with the customer or prospect in mind. What are *their* issues? What are their pain points or points of need? How can your company provide answers and solutions? Don't write that your MX-1000 can solve every problem under the sun. This isn't a marketing brochure.

Instead, share 10 best practice tips for managing thousands of acres of farmland; tip number 8 could then be a general tip that mentions the MX-1000 as an example of that solution.

Activity 1 (easy): Find and read two blog posts that are so compelling that you would complete an overly complex sharing process, including signing up for an e-mail newsletter, to share with your work colleagues.

Activity 2 (not as easy, but fun): Create 10 list-type blog post titles in the style of: 10 business blogging best practices, four ways an ergonomic desk chair helps employee morale, six steps to closing new business in 30 days.

2. *Create compelling audio content*—Written content is the most common type of content on a blog, but audio content can be easier to create. These can be reports from the field, interviews with product managers, or a short weekly update on industry news. There is a popular podcast where the two hosts meet once a week in a coffee shop and discuss the week's marketing news and events.

   Provide information that prospects can consume on the go and doesn't require a high level of attention to absorb. This can be a formal podcast, which can be downloaded automatically through a special RSS feed in iTunes, or an informal podcast, which can be downloaded manually from a blog post or just listened to on a computer. Treat this as special content that is regularly created and that has its own category on the blog. Once you are in the flow of recording audio podcasts regularly, consider adding a link to this category on the home page of your company website.

   BMC Software has worked with an outside provider to produce more than 250 audio podcasts since 2005. Each is 12 to 15 minutes long and features an interview with a BMC employee (communities .bmc.com/communities/blogs/bmcpodcasts).

   Activity 1: Pick two people in your organization or industry whom you have physical access to and whom you would like to interview.

   Activity 2: Test an audio recording with your smartphone and transfer it to your computer as an mp3 file.

3. *Create compelling video content*—Video is a great way to humanize a company. B2B buyers connect with people at companies they do business with. A short video of the customer service lead describing the most common troubleshooting techniques for a product is a great example of this. Trade show reports and trend interviews with industry leaders also make great video content. A weekly tip video works

too, but make sure there is a large collection of tips before starting to publish them so that it can be sustained over time.

The quality of video shot with a smartphone continues to improve, and it can be fine for on-the-go–type reports. A pocket-style video camera can be better for shooting in more controlled environments because it can easily attach to a tripod. Even a tabletop tripod produces a better shot than a shaky handheld shot, no matter how many TV shows adopt the shaky camera style of documentaries. Pay attention to lighting and sound so that the subject can be seen and heard. Some pocket cameras accept an external microphone to capture better sound and reduce background noise. People will watch bad video if the audio is good, but they won't watch sparkling video if they can't hear what is being said.

Humor in B2B online video was pioneered by Tim Washer when he was at IBM with his "Art of the Sale" clip on YouTube, starring an IBM sales vice president as himself.[2] Tim is now at Cisco, bringing his brand of comedy to routers, switches, and other very funny networking equipment.

Activity: List 10 best practice tips for your industry that can be shared in 10 individual videos of less than one minute.

4. *Create compelling visual content*—Many B2B companies have had success driving business with visual content like infographics. Joe Chernov, vice president of content marketing at Eloqua, says, "Infographics play multiple functions in our lead generation program. The first is, they address one of our biggest challenges: awareness. Because they speak to a broader group of marketers and are inherently sharable, infographics create the awareness needed to help us fill the top of the funnel. They attract new leads that we later nurture, score and route to sales using our own product. Infographics also result in more inbound links, blog post views, and social engagement than any other type of content.

"It's our infographics that have opened the door to press coverage on popular industry websites—historically hard nuts to crack for enterprise B2B vendors. We have also begun using infographics in our lead nurturing program to fill the gap between sign-up and first contact.

"And infographics correlate positively to sales. For example, 49 viewers of The Blog Tree (blog.eloqua.com/the-blog-tree/) infographic became customers. We see our blog as lightweight nurturing so a steady flow of interesting, topical, timely infographics is a way to keep our prospects engaged with us throughout the sales cycle."

5. *Create compelling mobile content*—Businesspeople spend more time on their mobile devices than ever before. Search and social media are going mobile, and prospects need to find what they are looking for in a format that is easily consumable on a mobile device. These are likely to be smartphones, but if your B2B company targets small businesses, it is likely that prospects still use feature phones.

   Determine what current content on your company website is relevant to the mobile visitor. Usually high-level information that moves a company into the consideration phase makes sense to be formatted for mobile phones. If the blog includes white papers and ebooks, whether as posts or calls to action, make sure they include short summaries so that mobile users can determine whether this information is useful in their search. This content needs share buttons, especially a share by e-mail button, so they can e-mail a link to this content to themselves and their colleagues. A blog also needs to be formatted for mobile viewing. Read more about mobile in Chapter 12.

   All blog content needs to be consumable on an iPad, the leading tablet. Most major video sites have switched to video formats that are compatible (HTML5) with iPhones and iPads. Make sure to use these embed codes when posting videos on your blog. If you have any doubts about which way this is going, Canaccord Genuity analyst T. Michael Walkley predicts sales of more than 100 million iPhones and more than 55 million iPads in 2012.[3]

   NetLine, an online lead generation company, expanded its TradePub.com site to mobile versions on the iPhone, BlackBerry, and iPad, with Android and Windows on the way. This app lets users download B2B content such as ebooks, white papers, and magazines directly to their mobile devices. Providers of the content receive the contact information from the users.

   Activity: List the five things on your website you think make sense for mobile content. Check your site analytics for the top five pages accessed by mobile devices.

6. *Curate content*—Blog content does not all have to be original, but at the same time, it should not be lifted wholesale from other sources without attribution. That is still called plagiarism in the online world, and not only do we not condone that, but it is not good for business.

   Publish one post per week that shares five recent and relevant posts or news articles from your industry. Develop a standard format that is easy to compile each week and determine whether the summaries of the posts include your comments and analysis or just the opening paragraph and links. These are frequently done on Friday as a weekly wrap-up, but we have also seen these posts on Monday as a way to kick off the week. Your process for inclusion in the post can be determined by popularity, recent posts about an industry topic, or posts that your audience may have missed.

Something you should not overlook is the title of this Friday post. Do not call it "Five Posts I Read and You Should Too." It should have a compelling, keyword-based, sharable title just like every other post. Something like: "Stunning Medical Devices That Will Change Your Life." The headline of the most important and compelling items works too.

Regularly searching Twitter for posts with your keywords and monitoring LinkedIn Groups and LinkedIn News pages are good regular sources for posts. A more advanced way to ensure an endless supply of content for these weekly curated posts is to add sources to a folder in an RSS reader, such as Google Reader. This makes it easy to search through a series of headlines from multiple blogs and news sources to find relevant posts.

Activity: List 10 sources that you could draw posts from on a weekly basis for a curated blog post.

7. *Post regularly*—Blogging is not a short-term activity; neither is growing a business or becoming a marketing superstar. You must make a major commitment to publishing quality content on an ongoing basis. This is unlike other marketing initiatives where there is a clear end point. Although you may determine some artificial end points for reporting purposes, you are always blogging. If sales should always be closing. Marketing should always be blogging.

Blogging is something that takes practice and the support of others. The nature of the Internet is that older posts have a long life span and continue to attract traffic. Posts that draw traffic continue to place high in search results, which means these older posts really do continue working. But that is dependent on the blog continuing to be updated and search engines seeing fresh content on the site. This is ideal for a tactic that is used to generate leads. Trade publication ads have a limited life span of driving traffic. Even digital display ads and pay-per-click ads have campaign life spans, mainly due to budget. But a great, keyword-rich blog post never expires and can continue to drive leads.

Activity: Choose a blog post topic for each week for the next four weeks. Determine a matching theme for a curated post and start watching for posts from others on that theme.

8. *Become an industry resource*—As trade publications fade away, there is a wide open opportunity for a B2B company to own its industry thought leadership with a blog. This goes way beyond the traditional idea of thought leadership to the idea of industry journalism. Combining some of the previous content suggestions, such as interviews with industry leaders, trade show reports, and curation of other industry content, you can now create a single destination where industry professionals can go to learn about the latest in your field. This is why it is important to populate a blog with information that is bigger than your company's solutions. It also positions your company as a resource, and one that is concerned with issues bigger than itself, which will drive a larger pool of readers and potential leads.

Activity: Name the two biggest trade shows in your industry and identify the industry leaders you would interview if you attended the show. Conduct the interviews by phone or e-mail, even if you don't attend the show.

9. *Include calls to action*—As we saw in Chapter 2, calls to action are how social media connects to the sales funnel. A blog post with a CTA is the content that gets a prospect to take action. Once someone arrives at a blog post about a topic, clicking on a CTA related to that topic is an easy next step if the post was of high quality. If a prospect is looking for a bar code provider and finds a blog post that describes an efficient means to bar coding incoming inventory, then that prospect is likely to click on a CTA to download an ebook about warehouse management. As blog leads become customers, you can analyze data to determine which topics and articles drive the most revenue; you can then incorporate more of those in your blogging strategy.

Can we be clearer?

Blog posts need calls to action.

HubSpot is one of the best B2B examples of using offers and calls to action on every blog post to drive leads. For example, if they publish a post about using Facebook Pages for business marketing, there is an offer to watch a recorded Facebook marketing webinar, as seen in Figure 7.4. Clicking on the link brings users to a form so that they can become a lead.

FIGURE 7.4 HubSpot includes Calls to Action on Every Blog Post

Driving traffic to show people how smart you are is a short-term strategy. Marketing superstars drive business through leads that are trackable. That's what we all want, right? Leads! Leads! Leads!

You'll have to read another book to discover what sales will do with those leads, but for now, let's generate them.

Activity: List two existing pieces of content and two pieces of content that you could create that can be used for calls to action to complement blog posts.

10. *Engage with readers*—There are two kinds of readers on a company blog: those who come to the blog to read the posts for information and those who come to the blog to read the posts for information related to a specific business purchase. Although we have focused on the second group as a means to generate leads, let's think about the first group now. It is likely they arrived by clicking on a link shared through social media, not search. It is important to engage with these readers and encourage them to take action as well. That action could be to leave a comment, but it is more likely to be to share the post content with their social networks. This action is important because it helps extend the reach of the content and gives prospects the opportunity to discover it. Use social media sharing

buttons on your blog and even ask readers in your post to share the article with their networks.

11. *Spread the content*—A blog is the center of a B2B social media approach to lead generation, but its mere existence doesn't mean it will attract prospects. Although an important aspect of the blog is to generate high search results, another way to influence that is to spread the content using your company social media profiles. There is certainly some efficiency in automating posting updates to your social media profiles, but it may make more sense to publish a blog post at one time and schedule updates to Twitter, Facebook, and LinkedIn at other times throughout the day. This depends on your audience and when they are active on social media sites.

    Share a blog post more than once on Twitter at different times of day, using different tweets. According to research by link shortener bitly, the half life of a shared link on Twitter, that is the amount of time it will get half the clicks it will ever get, is less than three hours.[4] The first tweet of a blog post should be automated with the post title, and the second one can be a variation on the title or a notable quote from the post. Share these links with a URL shortener that tracks clicks. This will allow you to compare the number of times a link was clicked with the number of times readers arrived at the blog. Capturing this data will let you know better times to update your networks.

12. *Leave comments*—One way to grow a company blog and create awareness for the blog throughout the industry is to leave comments on posts on other blogs in the industry. Do not leave irrelevant comments that don't add to the conversation of the post. Add only something of value. It is okay to leave a specific link if there is a blog post that is extremely relevant, but don't get overzealous with link sharing or the comment will be deleted as spam. And as a blog administrator, you will learn to hate blog spam, except when they are complete non sequiturs such as, "I'd like a packet of biscuits, please" (a real spam blog comment we received).

13. *Measure success*—When creating a blog to generate leads, the best measure of success is how many leads are generated; however, leads may not be generated from the start. This means other metrics need to be measured to show success. After launching a company blog, the number of posts per month is a metric worth tracking as you and the blog team learn to blog regularly.

Measuring traffic is also worth tracking in the beginning to establish a baseline. Traffic to a blog is an important metric because the number of leads generated can be shown as a percentage of traffic that shows up. As we discussed in Chapter 2, the two ways to increase the number of leads generated are to increase the traffic or increase the performance of the CTA. In the beginning, anything that can be tracked should be, but as things progress, it will be clear which metrics indicate success and which are no longer worth tracking.

14. *Optimize successful types of content*—On a blog that has a variety of content types, the feedback from traffic, leads generated, and ultimately, sales closed can help marketers understand what types of content drive traffic and what types of content drive leads. And be sure to consider mobile traffic in your optimization plans. Raw numbers are important, but understanding what kinds of content brings in not just leads but customers can help you optimize a blog to achieve its maximum success. It is still early enough in the history of social media that there are only a handful of companies that excel at using a blogging strategy to drive a significant number of leads and sales. Marketing superstars are the ones who pay attention to the right metrics and use that information to guide future plans, allowing their company to truly take advantage of social media lead generation.

15. *Guest blog posts*—There are two kinds of guest blog posts: ones that are written by others outside your company on your company blog and ones that you or others from your company write on other industry blogs. The first type does several things. These posts provide additional content to drive leads. You like that. It is also another way to promote others in the industry. This can get tricky in a small industry, as other writers could work for competitors. Seek out writers from trade publications, organizers of trade shows, and bloggers from other industries who could provide an outside perspective to a common industry issue. Once a blog becomes successful, expect to receive requests to publish guest posts.

The other type of guest post is where you reach out to other bloggers in the industry and write posts for their blogs. Be very clear on the type of post suggested, because the post cannot pitch a product or service and must provide some value to the readers of the blog. A link in a bio may be the only reference to your company.

LESSONS FROM A MARKETING SUPERSTAR

Name: Rick Short
Title: Director of Marketing Communications
Company: Indium Corporation
Years in Position: 10
What is your greatest social media/marketing success?
Okay, the first element of this success is increasing the QUALITY of my sales leads. When we shifted from an "outbound" philosophy to an "inbound" attitude, we emphasized the "long-tails" of our technologies. The result was a clear shift to opt-in, self-qualified, highly qualified, and urgent sales leads. They came to us as individuals who were eager and anxious to discuss highly technical, very detailed topics related to electronics assembly materials and assembly processes. Anecdotal evidence that this was a tremendous success became apparent when my support and sales team began being THANKED for following up on our opt-in engagements (downloading white papers, contacting our engineers, authors, and bloggers, etc.). Eventually, one of my sales leaders shared that, when our new class of social media sales leads came to his attention, he moved them to the top of his list, saying, "These are the best leads I've ever received."

The second element is much more quantifiable. It has to do with the QUANTITY of sales leads that we receive. Each time we tweak (improve) our inbound-style social media program, we are rewarded by earning sales leads at an increasingly higher rate. Our second major phase of improvement saw our opt-in, self-qualified sales leads increase by over 600 percent (from one quarter to the next). In the year following that, and after another adjustment to our program, our sales leads increased by another 100 percent. Remember, the leads are of increasingly higher quality as well. These increases in the rates of incoming (highly qualified) sales leads has forced us to reexamine our CRM system!

(continued)

(continued)

What is your biggest roadblock in executing your social media strategy? My biggest problem is myself. I need to understand that my exuberance and enthusiasm must be tempered by the realities of a much larger organization. Although I am highly focused on social media opportunities, developments, and legend, I have to continually remind myself that my business leaders have a myriad of other plates that they are spinning. To address this issue, I keep a very bright spotlight on our written GOAL and resist "mission creep" as much as possible. I use the mantra: *CONTENT* to *CONTACT* to *CASH*.

With anything digital, especially online and especially when it involves other people, it is easy to lose sight of the objective. There are so many alluring, sexy, and tempting distractions and alternatives out there. In the end, my dogmatic emphasis of the GOAL is appreciated by my teammates. They see that I am not swooning over each new piece of e-candy and that my goals are THEIR GOALS. In a sense, an overzealous social media marketer can be dangerous to a business unit leader. But a collegial, aligned, tightly focused social media guide can be a great asset. I remind myself of this daily.

What is the single most important trait of a B2B marketer? ALWAYS BEGIN AT THE END. This is my way of enforcing goal-oriented project management. Face it, we have so many dazzling tools at our fingertips that it is easy to simply start using them. I call such activities, "Art Projects." But, in the business realm, just because we have some construction paper, yarn, glitter, glue, and a few dried elbow macaronis, it doesn't mean we should start consuming them. We all know where these things end up: on the refrigerator. We also know that they are just as quickly taken down, put in a box, and never seen again.

Art Projects are insidious because they feel good and make us feel like we are making some sort of progress. In reality, they prevent us from aligning our resources into a super force that can be used to dominate the competition. By creating a goal, as a team, and by putting it into writing, we enable ourselves. By referring to that written goal throughout the program, we keep ourselves, and our organization, on track. This offers alignment, efficiency, and smoothness. Under such a situation, stress, misunderstandings, frustrations, and failures are greatly reduced. It all adds up to keeping my team as far away from "average" as we can get.

Blog Content Drives Leads

Whew, that was a lot of information. We broke it up into small chunks so that you can master business blogging at your own pace. The better a blog is planned and executed, the more likely it is to be found and read by your target personas. Remarkable content drives traffic, gets shared, drives more traffic, and gets shared some more. Success in social media breeds more success because of the network effect of socially networked individuals and the nature of Internet search engines.

When the right people arrive at your company blog, they actually want more information! What happens if there is not a CTA at the end of the post or in the sidebar to point them in the right direction?

Nothing.

B2B marketers often do a great job of driving traffic to a blog, but without a CTA on the post, or at least in the sidebar, there is no place for visitors to go. At that point they are likely to leave. Remarkable content without a payoff is not worth the effort.

Repeat after me: "Every blog post will have a CTA. Every blog post will have a CTA." Except for maybe the largest of B2B companies, social media is not about brand awareness. Many B2B companies do not have enough money to build a brand. They also don't have a large enough market to make it worth any amount of money. All marketing expenditures need to be evaluated based on their ability to drive leads and sales. A social media program with blogging at its center needs to be viewed through that lens.

Attract the target audience to the blog by providing helpful, valuable, and remarkable content. Click. They arrive at a landing page, fill out a form and become a lead. That is the goal of B2B blogging. Get them into the funnel today so that they can move into the consideration phase sooner and shorten the buying cycle. This reduces your cost per lead.

Three B2B Blogging Steps to Superstardom

1. *Get a head start*—Get ahead of the blogging game. The best way to start blogging is to start blogging. Write your first five blog posts before you launch your company blog. Starting eight weeks before the launch of your blog, spend two weeks developing at least 10 ideas for blog posts. Write one post a week for the next five weeks after that. You are now ready to take your blog live, you are five weeks ahead, and you understand how to fit a blog post per week into your schedule.

2. *Interview the experts*—There is tremendous knowledge within your company. Identify and interview two experts within your company in the next 60 days for the company blog. Try to find people from different areas who can share information about different parts of the company story. If you interview them on video, you have the opportunity to create multiple posts from the same interview. You can produce a written interview and several videos clips that can be published separately.

3. *Put a CTA in EVERY blog post*—Determine which ebooks or webinars you will promote on your company blog. Create text links or image-based calls to action to landing pages for these offers. If you have an existing company blog, take a few hours to add these calls to action to old posts. Remember that blogging is an annuity, and old posts generate leads too!

Become a LinkedIn Lead Generation Superstar

LinkedIn is known as the professional social network. It has been called Facebook with a suit and tie and Twitter on its best behavior. It is also the place business-to-business (B2B) marketers gain the most leads.

According to a June 2010 study by LeadForce1, now LeadFormix, LinkedIn drove more leads to B2B websites than any other site, and nearly three times the number as Twitter.[1] HubSpot reported that 61 percent of B2B companies using the social network have acquired a customer through LinkedIn.[2] This was the largest percentage of customer acquisition from social media sources, including the company blog. So LinkedIn has been proved to not just drive leads, but to convert leads to customers. If you uncover the secrets to success on this social network, you can continue on your path to superstardom.

In the ongoing battle between marketing and sales, LinkedIn can be a mighty tool to repair this rift. You can create opportunities for prequalified, inbound leads. As the sales force gains confidence in the quality of the leads, they will be more likely to accept leads from other social sources. The other role you can play is to identify other areas on LinkedIn, both generally and specifically, to find prospects and to begin conversations and connections.

Profiles Are Just the Beginning

LinkedIn started as a job search site where connections were made in the hopes of landing that dream job. This means that the core of the site is based around personal profiles and the networks people build. The best advice about a personal network is that you should always be building a network, especially when you do not need it. It will be more organic and authentic if it grows naturally.

Eight Tips for Growing a LinkedIn Network

Many people send LinkedIn requests to people they do not know. This creates a network of weak ties with few personal connections. It can be challenging to leverage that type of network, especially when looking for business connections that can lead to positive outcomes. The following tips can help you build a network of strong ties on LinkedIn, which helps generate business.

1. Follow an in-person meeting with a LinkedIn connection request.
2. Follow up on phone calls with a LinkedIn connection request. It is great to tell the person during the call that a LinkedIn request is coming when you hang up.
3. If you had an especially productive conversation on Twitter or Google+, send that person a LinkedIn request.
4. Do not use the generic request. Add some detail about the meeting or conversation, or your reason for connecting. Context is always better.
5. Import contacts from your e-mail to find both personal and business connections.
6. Review LinkedIn suggested connections and other network connections to find new connections.
7. Connect with all work colleagues, as it shows a strong impression of your connected company to prospects. There are company administrative functions that require a connection to other employees before a person can be added to certain fields. We'll get to those soon.
8. Reach out to others in your industry or target industries who are in the same LinkedIn Groups as you, but make sure you add context to the request.

Your Profile Can Work Harder for You

A fully realized profile should contain much more than just employment history and education, but even those sections can be optimized for discovery through search. This will let your profile work harder for you. Review the unified keyword list created in Chapter 3 to find just the right words to describe your current position and company. Search results happen both within LinkedIn and through outside search engines. The keywords can also be added to your profile's headline and summary to ensure your profile is found.

Every social media profile should have a photo, and LinkedIn is no exception. If your company website has staff photos, especially ones with a particular style or background, using that photo on your profile promotes your company brand and visually connects your profile to your company website.

Marketing superstars always have a few tricks up their sleeves that make them look good. This is one of them: the default category for website links on a profile is "Personal Website." Change the drop-down choice to "Other." This opens a customizable field to enter your company's name, or even descriptive keywords, that display as a link to the company website or blog. This personalizes a profile with your company name and demonstrates a higher level of knowledge to anyone visiting your profile. This does not provide any benefit for search engines, as many advise, but it gives a more polished look to your profile.

A LinkedIn Profile Is Not Like a Company Business Card

Companies design business cards and determine what information appears on them. They are part of a company's brand and image. Companies cannot dictate how an employee's profile looks on LinkedIn. The person, not the company, owns the personal profile. (It is, however, acceptable for a company to offer employees best practices and suggestions for consistent wording and applications showcasing company information on their profiles.)

There are plenty of resources available online about maximizing a LinkedIn profile for personal gain; however, we will not address that in this book. We are focusing on using LinkedIn for company benefit, generating leads and becoming a marketing superstar within an organization. But since much in the world of social media occurs in public, marketers who succeed frequently become known outside the company through guest blog posts, interviews, and public speaking.

Companies Can Get Recommendations Too

The ability for companies to create a compelling profile on LinkedIn has continued to grow. Before the addition of company pages, clicking on a company link meant launching a search for other employees in that company. Now, in most cases, clicking on the company in a person's profile leads to a company page, as seen in Figure 8.1. Companies are no longer a collection of individuals on LinkedIn. With the addition of status updates they can share content and express a point of view.

Your company can now begin to create a branded experience on LinkedIn. The top of a company page contains a logo and an overview of the company. This is basic branding that should describe your company using the appropriate keywords. There is nothing too groundbreaking here, but LinkedIn collapses the description so that visitors to this page can view the reason they are there. That's the list of people who work at the company, sorted by degree of connections. We will get back to the people in just a bit, but we are not done at the top.

The Careers tab shows company jobs. When a company posts a paid job listing on LinkedIn, it can treat the job like an offer. If a company has

FIGURE 8.1 Salesforce.com LinkedIn Company Profile

a job or jobs that it needs to fill and the pool of applicants is on LinkedIn, the object is to get the job listing in front of as many potential employees as possible. Encourage other company employees to share the job posting with their networks.

Prospective employees at the top of the funnel are all those who respond and say they are interested. The list gets winnowed down just like leads get qualified. The difference is that a company may be looking for only one person to fill a position, but it would be looking for multiple customers.

And now for the Products & Services tab. This is where the power of leads on the company page comes from, whether your company is looking to drive leads or to seek out leads. Start by adding your company's products and services to this tab, because this is where company recommendations go. Let me repeat that. Company recommendations go on individual products and services, so companies that *don't* have products or services listed cannot get any recommendations.

Complete product and services listings as much as possible, especially the contact information. These can generate direct leads from prospects interested in that product. Each product listing has a permalink, or its own address, so it can be shared with others on LinkedIn as an update or in a direct message. The listing can also be shared on Twitter.

Awareness of a product is created by repeated exposure to various versions of the message. Ask employees and customers to share these links as well. It's possible to add a relevant message to the update, which means it's possible to add value in addition to the product link. Then be sure to ask your customers to become brand advocates for you and leave a recommendation.

For example, Salesforce.com has 10 products listed and 790 recommendations. Each one of these recommendations is a customer letting others know that they use a Salesforce.com product and are happy with it. Many of these recommendations have no additional comments, but the ones that do, provide some context to the recommendation.

These brand advocates need to be encouraged. They need to be identified and matched up with customer records in the customer relationship management (CRM) system. Make sure this information filters down to the appropriate company salesperson. These advocates also need to be thanked and rewarded. These are the customers to consider for a customer council to provide feedback on current and future products. Everyone likes to get inside information, and people who have publicly stated they recommend a product are prime candidates.

Competitors will also have product listings and recommendations. Review their customers to see who has made recommendations and provide those names to the sales team as your competitor's brand advocates. Depending on the nature of the business, they may not be leads at all. Purchasers of complex B2B products may not even be interested in the products of a competitor, but awareness is where it starts. A salesperson can make note of the contact and file it away for future use. If the person is active on LinkedIn, it might be possible to know what events he or she attends, giving the salesperson the opportunity to arrange a short meeting.

Just like a journey begins with one step, a B2B sale begins with a connection.

Business Value Through Sharing

Providing value to connections is key to business success in social media. LinkedIn is no different. Companies can share content on their profile, with company status updates and importing blog and Twitter feeds. The status update has already been seen as a way to drive quality and target leads to blog posts and landing pages.

Personal status updates are not like a Facebook update. It is not about the song you are currently listening to or sharing photos. Updates on LinkedIn should be business focused. To see what types of updates people share, go to the LinkedIn News sections, which aggregate stories shared by members of LinkedIn.

It is also easy to connect Twitter to a LinkedIn profile. Generally, it is a good idea to do so, but do not push every tweet to LinkedIn. One way to manage this is to set your Twitter account to push only those tweets that contain #in to your LinkedIn account. Although it can be easy to forget to add the #in hashtag, it's better than the alternative of posting too many irrelevant updates to your professional network, which could easily overwhelm your connections.

Another approach is to add LinkedIn personal profiles updates to TweetDeck or HootSuite and then selectively update from those social media management programs. Sharing information on LinkedIn can be handled just like posting on other social profiles. Develop an editorial calendar that is topic driven and indicates how often company information is published and when third-party articles are shared. Use the 10-4-1 rule for social sharing. That is, for every 10 updates from third-party sources, publish four company updates and one link to a landing page. See more about this rule in the next chapter.

The calendar also needs to be coordinated among several people at your company with significant networks. Decide on a frequency that makes sense for each person, and start slowly if the people haven't posted much content to LinkedIn.

This is where a marketing superstar must be strong when people claim this is not an authentic approach. You are on LinkedIn to generate strong networks for company employees so that you can generate leads. Why is an organized plan a problem? You are seeking positive business outcomes from your social media endeavors. Planning helps that happen.

Grouping Your Expertise: LinkedIn Groups

Connecting with a group of people who share a common interest is a powerful way to drive business. Whatever the industry, there are several, or tons, of LinkedIn Groups with relevant discussions that are worth following. Under the Groups tab, LinkedIn offers suggestions for groups that might interest you. The more complete a person's profile is, the more on point these suggestions are—another reason to be as complete as possible. It is also possible to browse and search for groups that might contain prospects.

Another way to find groups that might yield business results is to review the group memberships of your connections. This is another reason why it is important to build a network of real contacts.

There are two kinds of groups on LinkedIn: open and closed. Anyone can join open groups, but prospective members of closed groups must be reviewed and approved by the manager of the group. This is meant to keep spammers out of groups, but most people are approved.

Like so many other aspects of social media, begin group membership as a lurker. It is not possible to review the relevance of many groups before joining, so upon joining, it makes sense to click through all the discussions and feeds to see what the members are talking about and how they are interacting. Many groups, especially some of the largest ones, are filled with self-promotion. That is not the goal of joining a group. The goal is to provide value to other members by sharing expertise and resources.

This will ultimately lead to building connections, driving traffic to landing pages for deeper educational content, and obtaining indirect leads derived from others checking out your profile or the profiles of other company employees.

Eric Blumthal, chief executive officer (CEO) of count5, a sales training software company, answered a question in a group on LinkedIn. After visiting Eric's profile, the CEO of a 300-person company wanted to talk with him because the CEO was interested in count5's technology. Count5 had a buy decision in less than a week and a contract two weeks later, compared with count5's normal sales cycle of six to nine months. And the answer Eric provided in the group discussion had nothing to do with his product. He was just sharing his experience.

You, the rising marketing superstar, can play a scouting or lookout role when it comes to LinkedIn Groups. You are the perfect person within a B2B company to identify the groups worth joining and perhaps even monitor discussion threads with the in-depth knowledge of what is relevant. But when it comes to commenting and sharing knowledge, there may be other specialists within your organization who are better suited to that role.

For this to be a successful approach to maximizing leads from LinkedIn Groups, people need to commit to participating in the groups. Every group, no matter the size, has a core of regular contributors and most active members. Interacting with those group leaders, responding to their questions, and making connections is one of the quickest ways to becoming a key member of the group.

Instead of joining an existing group, many B2B marketers start their own company-sponsored group. This is not a recommended first-step approach. Before starting your own group, spend time in other groups and watch how a well-managed group runs. A new group needs to recruit members, have an active community manager, have an industry focus that is larger than the sponsoring company, and have an editorial calendar, or plan, to keep the group membership active with information to comment on.

Being a member of a group is like going to the grocery store to find items on a shopping list. Starting and running your own group is the equivalent of running a grocery store, which requires constant stocking and maintenance. Ensure you can commit resources before starting a LinkedIn Group.

For another example of the power of LinkedIn Groups to generate leads we look to Kodak. Not the consumer side of the iconic camera maker, but the professional side of the business that caters to commercial printers. Kodak created a conference presentation to promote awareness of its customers' award-winning work produced on Kodak's digital presses. Following that presentation at an industry conference, Mark Egeling, segment marketing director of Americans with Kodak, wrote a blog post that recounted some of the key points in the presentation and offered a free return on investment (ROI) calculator that printers could share with their customers.[3] Links to this post were shared in more than 20 different groups geared to printers. Of those arriving at the landing page from LinkedIn, 45 percent provided their basic contact information and became new leads.

Answering the Questions: LinkedIn Answers

A much more free-form area to demonstrate expertise, share information, and build enough awareness of a company to get prospects to the top of the funnel is the question and answer section called LinkedIn Answers. These are organized by category but are searchable by keywords, across all categories or within a category.

Again, just like with group discussions, you, the marketer, can discover the questions and share them with other experts within your organization to provide answers. LinkedIn rewards users who answer a lot of questions, but note that users can provide a maximum of 50 answers within a 24-hour period. The person who asks the question can indicate the best answer, and the people who provided the answer get an expert point. The most active answerers can not only flaunt their expertise but also gain business from their activity. They are featured on the Answers home page and on category pages as leading experts on those subjects. Did you even know that gaming aspects and the competition created by a leader board existed within LinkedIn?

Asking questions can also yield business results. This can be a source of research to obtain answers to questions, obviously, but it can also be a way to share a point of view that represents a company. For example, it is okay for an employee of a social media monitoring company to ask a question such as, "What free tools do you use to monitor your company's social media efforts? And what paid tools have you considered?" It is too self-promotional for the same employee to ask, "Have you tried our latest release of product X?" LinkedIn recommends that questions be descriptive and concise.

Some of the examples in this chapter came from asking questions on LinkedIn. It seemed like the right thing to do.

Aaron Corson is in charge of business development for St. Louis printer NJC Printing. He responded with his contact information to the following request posted on LinkedIn Answers: "I'm looking for a printer for high quality marketing materials. Does anyone have a recommendation?" Within 45 minutes he received a request for a project bid in his e-mail, which he immediately responded to. It is a small job, but he expects to do additional business with the company if he gets the project. In the printing industry, the bid-to-sale ratio is about 10 to 20 percent.

Aaron spends some time on LinkedIn prospecting and looking for leads. He imports LinkedIn Answers feeds into his Google Reader, so he can easily see questions across all of the categories he follows. He answers one or two questions a week to demonstrate his printing expertise by sharing helpful information. Most questions are not specific requests for service providers.

Anyone can answer questions about any topic; the only requirement is that the user has a LinkedIn profile. When someone asks a question, it shows up in his or her activity stream, allowing connections to see the question being asked. Questions can also be sent to specific connections if they will likely provide a good answer. Each question also has a permalink, so it can be shared outside of LinkedIn to solicit answers from those across other social networks. Questions and selected answers can be used as research for blog posts to share the wisdom of the crowd with followers of your company.

Professionals Need Advertising Too

LinkedIn offers businesses several opportunities to advertise on their platform. Large brands can contact LinkedIn directly for customized programs, and there is a self-service system for everyone else. Users create a business profile to start, and then enter the ad copy, upload a logo, and determine a daily budget for their pay-per-click ads. When LinkedIn serves these ads, they can appear in the sidebar or in the footer of the page. They can even appear in the header as text ads. It is not possible to specify any of these details so make sure each of these elements can stand alone.

Argyle Social, makers of a social media marketing dashboard, launched its product with pay-per-click, keyword-based ads on Google. Like any marketing campaign, it was not the only tactic that they were counting on to drive business, but every component needed to work as hard as possible. After a trial period of disappointing results, they focused their paid advertising on LinkedIn for two main reasons. Eric Boggs, cofounder and CEO, wanted to lower the cost of leads and make sure they were well targeted.

LinkedIn ads were an order of magnitude cheaper than Google ads for Argyle and the company could target customers much more precisely based on job title, company size, level in the organization and LinkedIn Group membership. Argyle's initial offers were for a demo or a free trial to try its software platform. Although this brought good results, when the company changed the offer to download a white paper about social media ROI, leads skyrocketed in both number and quality. Changing the offer created a larger pool of potential leads, as the company was now targeting prospects higher up in the buying process, people at the top of the funnel. These were people raising their hands and expressing interest, rather than expressing their intent to commit to a social media solution.

Because of the precise targeting available on LinkedIn, Argyle was able to hone in on who its prospects really were. By continuing to tweak the targeting, the company has gotten closer and closer to its pool of prospects. Argyle is now achieving a click to lead rate of 25 percent.

Eric's advice to anyone looking at LinkedIn advertising is to start with your customer and prospect profile and begin targeting people like that. These types of campaigns need to continue to be monitored and iterated. As a software start-up, it is in their DNA to constantly make changes to continually improve. LinkedIn's advertising program offers many different knobs to turn to fine-tune the approach.

Our hope is that after implementing ideas from this and other chapters in the book you will feel comfortable adding marketing superstar to your LinkedIn profile. Please let us know when you do, and we can feature you and your successes online or in a future publication.

Three B2B LinkedIn Steps to Superstardom

1. *Complete your company profile*—A completed company profile is key to lead generation on LinkedIn. Over the next 30 days, commit to completely filling out the Company page, including adding the Twitter and blog feeds and adding a full complement of products. If a video is not available for each product, make one that is one to two minutes long.

2. *Join a group*—You can find a group for any industry, topic, or interest. Identify 10 groups to join based on your target prospects. Join the groups and monitor the conversation for a month to determine how to add value with content. Building thought leadership within the group creates connections and introductions that foster leads and sales. Recommend high-value groups to others in the company and encourage them to join and share company content as well.

3. *Organize LinkedIn sharing*—Sharing content on LinkedIn is key. However, it is important to be organized in your approach. Develop an editorial calendar for one month that outlines status updates for the company and individual topics and group discussion threads. Coordinate this schedule with three people from your company to ensure that you are all coordinated in building LinkedIn reach and leads.

Twitter

Leads in 140 Characters

Even though Twitter started as a status update service, it quickly became much more than that when users made it their own. Marketing superstars understand the power of sharing, which is where Twitter excels. They also understand the idea of keeping it simple.

"Twitter's core concept is the extension of simple, short messages throughout the past many decades," wrote M. G. Siegler on TechCrunch. "The postcard begat the SMS message begat the IM status message begat Twitter. Sometimes the simplest ideas resonate because of the very fact that they are simple."[1]

The magic of Twitter was its simplicity, but the thing that allowed the platform to really grow was its asynchronous nature. Users could follow any other user without approval, and this is what drove the growth of media and celebrity profiles. This means that your company account can discover and follow prospects online, which we will discuss more later in this chapter, without those users needing to approve the follow.

Many business-to-business (B2B) companies have struggled with Twitter because they don't understand what to do on the platform. It is so simple that it is hard for some to know where to start. One way to start is to spend 10 minutes every morning searching for industry-related terms. These searches can also be automated using a variety of tools, such as TweetDeck or HootSuite, or they can be done manually using Twitter search. Use this regular, daily search to show colleagues and executives that people are talking about your industry online.

Five Off-Platform Benefits of Twitter

If you discover that your customers and prospects are not on Twitter, here are five benefits of being there anyway. Laura Fitton, coauthor of *Twitter For Dummies,* described these benefits[2]:

1. *Search engine optimization (SEO)*—If your Twitter account is your company name, as it should be, every tweet and @reply provides a link to your company name. Twitter is also a source of frequently updated and relevant content that is used by search engines in their search results for a keyword.

2. *Content generation engine*—Companies can use Twitter to provide updates and share articles, even if no one is following them. A widget of your Twitter feed can be placed on your website with a live feed that updates from Twitter. Imagine being able to share important short updates from a major industry event right on your home page, in real time. You can with Twitter.

3. *Research tool*—Companies can conduct two kinds of research on Twitter. The first is passive, where they search, listen, and monitor for relevant information that can help their business. The second is active, where they can ask specific questions to a Twitter audience and record the answers.

4. *Word of mouth and pass along*—Companies have proved that word of mouth spreads across Twitter and off the platform. The pass along value of information is high on the network, but it also bleeds out into the real world with results. For example, Scania Group (twitter.com/scaniagroup), a producer of heavy commercial trucks, has amassed more than 4,000 Twitter followers by sharing content related to fuel consumption reduction and driver safety.

5. *PR gravity*—People and companies on Twitter that engage in smart conversations, share quality content, and demonstrate a knowledge and value to their industry can easily be contacted by journalists looking for credible sources. Publishers of industry newsletters always need content, and if you have been providing solutions to business problems, you have positioned yourself to be contacted.

Anatomy of a Tweet

Since we frequently encounter marketers who don't understand all the details of Twitter, here is an introduction. See Figure 9.1 for a view of the Twitter stream, showing the most recent tweets from the user's followers. If you are well versed in the Twittersphere, skip ahead to the Finding Leads section. You have our permission.

A tweet, a message posted on Twitter, is limited to 140 characters, and that limit is derived from its SMS, or text message, origins. Text messages are limited to 160 characters; Twitter decided on 140 characters, leaving the remaining 20 characters for user names.

An analysis of tweets by Sysomos has shown that 15 percent of tweets contain links to other content.[3] The inclusion of links is one of the unintended developments of Twitter. As users began sharing content on the platform, the rise of URL shorteners like bitly accelerated, saving precious characters by creating permanent short link redirects to the content that is shared. Bitly, and other URL shorteners, track the number of clicks on a link.

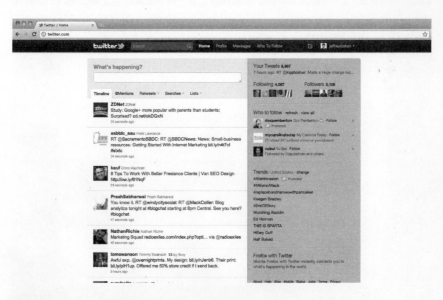

FIGURE 9.1 Twitter User Home Page

Replies and Mentions

A tweet that begins with a user's Twitter ID, including the @ symbol, is called a reply, and it is used when replying directly to someone. An example is below in Figure 9.2. A reply tweet is seen by a user's followers only if they also follow the person being replied to. To keep all tweets visible in followers' streams begin the tweet with another word, such as "hey" or "hi," or even another character, such as a period or an asterisk. Reply tweets are also excluded from Twitter lists.

A Twitter mention is a tweet that contains a Twitter ID preceded by the @ symbol somewhere in the message besides at the beginning. Companies need to monitor Twitter to make sure they see tweets with their Twitter ID in them. The Twitter website has a tab showing these mentions. Many third-party applications allow you to add a column to show these tweets separately from the home feed of tweets. Exercise your marketing superstar skills by enabling push notifications on your smartphone to get real-time alerts of these mentions when you are away from your computer.

FIGURE 9.2 Example of Twitter Reply

Retweets

A retweet is a tweet from one user that has been shared by a second user. This is a common way to share posts or articles from an authoritative source. For example, rather than writing a tweet to share an article from a trade magazine, a user can retweet the publication's tweet. There are two ways to retweet. The better method shows the tweet coming from the retweeter and references the original tweeter. This is the top example in Figure 9.3. This method allows you to edit the original tweet or add your own comments.

The method favored by Twitter is to use their retweet function, which reposts the original tweet to the retweeter's followers, as seen in the bottom example in Figure 9.3. Many thiry party Twitter applications allow

FIGURE 9.3 Two Kinds of Twitter Retweets (The top example is seen as posted by the retweeter and includes RT to indicate that it is a retweet. The bottom example using Twitter's retweet function and appears to be posted by the original poster.)

users to choose which method they prefer. This second method can cause some confusion when followers see a tweet in their stream from a user they don't follow. It is also not as obvious who retweeted it, because the Twitter ID may appear in small type. One reason to retweet messages on Twitter is to share those messages with your followers. One of the principles of social media marketing is to share valuable information and receive credit for it from your followers. The first method makes it more obvious who is responsible for sharing the information.

Direct Messages

A direct message is a private message sent from one Twitter user to another. The second user must follow the first for this to work. These messages are not seen by other users, so it is a good way to ask for a prospect's phone number or other direct contact information. Do not share extremely private information over direct messages; they may pass through a third-party application, and all information is stored in Twitter's database.

Hashtags

A hashtag is a word or phrase preceded by a hash symbol (#). See an example tweet in Figure 9.4 with the hashtag #smb2b at the end of the tweet. These are used to connect conversations around a topic or event,

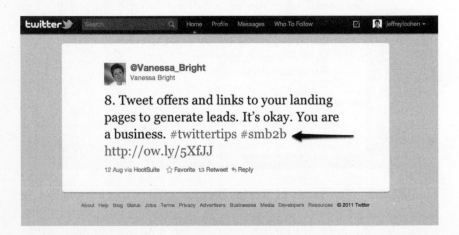

FIGURE 9.4 Example of Twitter Hashtag

or even to highlight a company or industry. Many businesses use these incorrectly by always including #companyname in tweets. If no one is searching for the hashtag, it provides no value to the tweets. Also, many industry hashtags are overused, or even used by spammers, which means there are too many tweets in the search results for your tweets to stand out and be read. In a study by Argyle Social, they found tweets with hashtags received 5 percent fewer clicks than those without.[4]

Finding B2B Leads on Twitter

According to a 2011 study from Edison Research, Twitter has nearly universal awareness in the United States, with 92 percent of Americans surveyed having heard of Twitter. However, only 8 percent of adult Americans have profiles on Twitter. Of those on the service, 3 in 10 Twitter users access the service daily and 7 of 10 have ever posted updates. Twitter is largely a network of working-age professionals; nearly 60 percent of monthly users are between 25 and 54 years old.[5]

When you are looking for B2B leads on Twitter, you have many tools to choose from. These tools can help you find prospects based on the information they are publicly providing in tweets. To start, go to Twitter.com and enter a single general search term or phrase that represents your company's product or industry. Once the search results come up, review them for relevance to the original search.

Click refine results to go to advanced search to exclude terms that are not relevant. For example, Twitter has many job listing feeds that come up in searches, which can be excluded by adding job in the None of these words field. If your company's products or services are offered locally, add information in the places field. It is also possible to find leads for a regional sales force using this same field by specifying a distance from a particular location.

Although this is a good one time search, to search for these keywords regularly, use a free program such as TweetDeck or HootSuite and add a column with this search. If you need more features to manage a team workflow of tweets, HootSuite, and CoTweet are available in enterprise versions for a fee. Larger companies might want to consider more robust paid social media monitoring systems such as Radian6 and Sysomos. Whichever way you choose, the power of searching Twitter for leads will be enhanced by an organized process and the appropriate resources of people and technology.

And by the way, search for a company name in a search engine and see if their Twitter profile comes up. Search again with the word Twitter included in the search string. If it still does not come up, the company does not have a Twitter profile or it has a Twitter name that does not relate to the company name. A Twitter account name may not seem like content, but in the world of inbound marketing, everything that helps a company get found and attract traffic counts.

Setting Up a B2B Twitter Account

Start with Two Names

When signing up for a Twitter account, companies should use their company name for their Twitter ID. Twitter user names can be 15 characters long. If that is not long enough, the real name field can be 20 characters long. If the company name is not descriptive, some B2B companies have considered adding keywords to either the ID or their real name.

A complete company name is usually the preferred real name of the account, but MarketingProfs chief content officer, Ann Handley, took a different path. She established the @MarketingProfs Twitter account in what would be described as according to best practices. Both the Twitter ID and real name of the account were MarketingProfs and the avatar, or icon, was the MarketingProfs logo. The more she used Twitter and understood the nature of the community, this approach didn't seem right. She changed the logo to a picture of herself and changed the real name to her own name. Not only did this feel right to Ann, but followers felt more comfortable talking to her directly. She has grown the @MarketingProfs Twitter account to more than 100,000 followers by literally becoming the face of the company on Twitter.[6]

Create a Descriptive Bio

A company's Twitter bio needs to strike the right balance between describing what the company does and using the words prospects are searching for. The extremes of this do not serve any company well. Do not choose the humorous approach of "Tweeting so you don't have to." Using all 160 characters, jam-packed full of keywords, not even separated by commas or spaces is not any better. A Twitter bio needs to be readable by humans and machines. As we said, balance is key.

To include a link in the Twitter bio, it must contain the full domain name with the http:// preceding it. Other Twitter management applications such as TweetDeck do convert URLs to live links without the http:// prefix. Twitter IDs in a bio are live links to Twitter accounts, and hashtags link to Twitter search results.

Let's go back to our example of Scania mentioned earlier in this chapter. Their Twitter bio reads: "The latest news from Scania Group, the leading manufacturer of heavy trucks and buses as well as industrial and marine engines." This is an example of a clear and effective B2B Twitter bio. It mentions the keywords heavy trucks and marine engines, while making sense to a person who would be interested in following the account.

Provide One Link

Twitter offers a single field for website link. This should be the company home page, with a clear call to action (CTA), or a landing page that is located at mycompany.com/twitter. Many companies use short URLs to gain click data, but some people are less likely to click on links if they don't know where they are going. The click data from URL shorteners is not always accurate. The best way to track this incoming traffic is to use a unique landing page that receives traffic only from that single Twitter link. This way you can be sure that number of unique visitors are the number of people who came from Twitter.

Let's go back to the home page before we move on. When someone clicks on the link in a Twitter profile, it is generally because he or she was intrigued by the tweets, name, or bio and wants to learn more. Make sure the user lands on a page where he or she can learn more. Don't repeat the same bio; rather, share a little more. Also give the user the opportunity to raise a hand and identify himself or herself as a lead. The path to do this must clear, whether on the home page or on a landing page. Remember, we are on Twitter for leads, not lunch.

The 10-4-1 Rule of Social Sharing

Providing consistent and frequently updated content on social networks is the key to expanding reach and generating leads. With so much information on so many channels, prospects are looking for sources to curate quality content, rather than having to wade through tweet after tweet of mindless chatter. By combining a variety of content in the right ratio, your company can serve that role.

Look to include content that is automatically tweeted from outside industry sources, company updates, or offers that link to landing pages.

The following is a ratio of content that maintains consistent flow of information with enough frequency for prospect engagement. Use this ratio on your company's social channels. We call this the 10-4-1 rule.

For every 10 tweets with links to articles from third-party sources, tweet 4 times with company updates or blog posts and 1 link to a company landing page.

It is important to apply this ratio for maximum impact no matter how often your company tweets per day. Tweets that are in direct response to other users are not counted in this ratio.

14 Ways to Drive Leads with Content on Twitter

1. *Tweet company blog posts*—If a blog is the hub of your company's social media presence, then the most obvious way to extend the reach of those posts is to tweet them to your company's followers. Tweet each blog post at least two times per day, using different words to attract different targets. The first tweet should be posted automatically with Twitterfeed or a similar tool when the post is published. Test posting at different times of day, and take global prospects into account when posting these tweets. This is also the most direct way to drive traffic back to your company website. Encourage employees to share these posts from their Twitter accounts for additional reach. Blog posts that include calls to action become lead-capturing machines. Building a Twitter following of targeted prospects makes the readers of the blog more qualified and more likely to become a lead.

2. *Like a Facebook page*—Many companies use both Twitter and Facebook to build their audiences for their content. Promote each platform on the other. The first step in creating an impression on

Facebook is to ask someone to like the company page. Make that request on Twitter to drive some additional prospects to Facebook.

Even though the Fluke Corporation, a manufacturer of test and measurement equipment, has five times the number of Facebook fans as Twitter followers, they use Twitter to promote Facebook. "We're almost 10K strong over at our FB page! Have you checked it out? We're giving away free stuff!" It doesn't hurt that they are giving away free stuff.[7]

3. *Promote your e-mail newsletter*—Tweet a link to your e-mail newsletter sign-up page with the same frequency as you send your e-mail. For example, if you send weekly e-mails, tweet the sign-up reminder weekly. If you send monthly e-mails, remind your Twitter followers monthly. It doesn't need to be more complicated than reminding followers that they can keep up with your company by subscribing. If there is room in the tweet, offer a bit of what they can expect from the regular e-mail. Providing more touch points (Twitter and e-mail) for prospects increases the likelihood of their becoming a lead.

4. *Share third-party articles of value*—B2B companies need to share more than their own content to be successful on Twitter. Seek out others in the industry and retweet their posts. Retweet your prospects' and customers' tweets to show your interest. Follow the 10-4-1 rule described previously and make sure you have enough industry sources to tweet 10 times for every four company updates.

5. *Direct followers to a landing page*—In the world of lead generation and compelling offers, you should tweet the offer with a link directly to the landing page. As we said in Chapter 2, even though social media "experts" may cringe, no puppies will die in the tweeting of the offer. The 10-4-1 rule guides the frequency of tweets to landing pages. If you have created a piece of content with the target persona in mind, the content will attract that target. Do not fear backlash from your followers. Instead plan to count the leads in your monthly report.

6. *Share a video*—If a picture is worth a thousand words, then one minute of Web video, which is generally 15 frames per second, is worth 900,000 words. And if that video conveys one compelling idea and has a CTA at the end with a clickable link, what is that worth to

your company? It could start sounding like dollars. Twitter easily allows sharing of video for both desktop and mobile devices. A short, remarkable tweet with a link to an embedded video will drive traffic. Notable B2B videos have included rapping interns, singing marketers, a bathroom snorting Euro model, computer salesmen, a day of glass, and stable routers that make gifts for all occasions.

7. *Optimize for keywords*—Twitter does not exist in a vacuum of its own Internet. Every tweet lives in a world where every page is indexed by multiple search engines. Each tweet is a page on the Internet. Companies need to use appropriate keywords in their tweets so that they will show up in customers' and prospects' searches. This doesn't mean every tweet needs keywords, but many of them should be optimized. Don't worry. This is not as difficult as it may sound. Tweeting company blog posts and articles from other sources that are relevant to the audience will already contain many of these keywords.

8. *Run a contest*—Using Twitter to spread the word about a contest is a great way to expand the reach of a message. Frequently companies hold contests that they hope will spread beyond their current audiences by giving away computers, iPads, or some other new gadgets, but targeted contests are more successful for B2B companies. A contest needs to relate to a company's business and its target audience. For contest entrants to be considered leads, they need to be targeted prospects.

   Digi-Key, distributor of electronic components, runs a variety of contests through their Twitter profile. In a trivia contest with a 30-minute time limit, they asked, "According to the UCS Satellite Database, how many operating satellites does the U.S. currently have in orbit around the earth?" Three winners won a variety of items—notebooks, coasters, and pens—with the Digi-Key logo on them.[8] They appealed to their technical customers and provided prizes that people would use on their desk.

9. *Share an ebook or white paper*—Companies create ebooks to share their knowledge and industry best practices. A well-designed collection of blog posts makes the perfect ebook. Publish an enhanced transcript of a webinar or a conference trend report as an ebook, and then use Twitter to let your industry know about the availability of these resources.

Traditional B2B marketing has always included the distribution of white papers, but the awareness of these documents was dependent on prospects finding their own way to a company website. Twitter now allows marketers to share these resources with interested people.

10. *Schedule tweets linking to evergreen content*—If your company has been blogging for a while, you have accumulated relevant posts that can be shared regularly. Blog posts about best practices or how-to posts can still be tweeted six months later. Traffic to a website or blog comes from a variety of sources, and one way to continue to drive traffic is to leverage older posts. People talk about the real-time nature of the Web and that the life span of a tweet is very short. It's been reported that 92 percent of retweets happen in the first hour after a tweet is posted.[9] This is why marketers need to resurface older content.

11. *Promote and conduct a webinar*—B2B companies that produce webinars can let their followers know about the event. By using targeted keywords, their tweets can reach others interested in the topic being presented. The broader and more relevant to industry professionals the webinar is, the more likely they are to attend and share the event with their Twitter following. Do not conduct a webinar that is a disguised sales pitch; that will not gain much interest. Rather, include one or two experts from outside of the company to add credibility to the presentation. Outside contributors can also help promote the webinar to their own Twitter followings to bring additional awareness to the event.

Every person who signs up for the webinar is a lead and should be treated that way. Follow best practices and include an opt-in box before adding these people to any regular communication list. Since the webinar is promoted on Twitter, include a place in the form for users to list their Twitter IDs; this will allow you to match their contact information with their Twitter profile for promotions on the platform.

During the webinar, include a unique hashtag so that users can share appropriate nuggets of information with their followers. During a HubSpot webinar about the science of social media, people were live tweeting the data shared in the webinar, like the best times of day to tweet. This presented HubSpot as the leader in providers of social media data. More than 25,000 people signed up for this webinar to watch it live or watch a recording afterward. These results are not typical for most B2B companies, but this company was able to obtain them because it has been producing and sharing a wide variety of content for years.

12. *Twitter chat*—Twitter chats are an ideal way to connect with others in your industry or with others with similar interests. These chats occur at a set time each week and usually last for one hour. A moderator asks a series of questions about a specific topic, and the participants answer the questions and have side conversations with others. All of this is managed by using the same hashtag. Sites like TweetChat.com can make it easier to participate in a Twitter chat by showing you only tweets with the hashtag and automatically appending the hashtag onto outgoing tweets. A good one to start with is the one about B2B marketing called #b2bchat. Check it out on Thursday at 8 PM U.S. Eastern Time.

13. *Respond to brand mentions*—The most obvious approach to Twitter lead generation, which is why it is here near the end, is responding to prospects who tweet using a company's Twitter ID. This is the equivalent of someone saying, "Hey, company X, I am interested in your products and I want to know more." Companies must have monitoring processes in place to discover these tweets and respond to these people. Assigning someone in your organization the responsibility of clicking on the @mentions tab on Twitter.com may not be enough. And you need to respond in a helpful way, rather than a sales way; however, when someone asks for more information, it is appropriate to respond with what he or she asked for.

14. *Listen for industry terms*—In addition to setting up discovery processes for tweets mentioning the company and product names, you need to set up searches to listen for industry terms, competitors, industry events, and general phrases that relate to company offerings. Although it makes sense to start with free tools such as Twitter search or other searches within Twitter applications, such as TweetDeck or HootSuite, the volume of these types of searches will be greater than company and product name searches and may require a paid solution to properly manage the amount of data coming in.

Five Ideas for Prospect Engagement for B2B Companies

1. *Ask a question about an upcoming event*—Twitter is a conversational medium, and asking questions of followers can generate interactions. If your company is attending a trade show or conference or hosting or sponsoring a social media event, ask attendees questions about the upcoming event. Questions about restaurants, activities, or show events are more likely to elicit a response. If the event has a hashtag, be sure to use it to reach nonfollowers. Making simple connections on Twitter is the first step to business connections and leads.

2. *Tweet a photo*—According to a study by Sysomos, 1.25 percent of all tweets include a link to a shared photo.[10] Sharing a photo on Twitter can show prospects the details within a company that they could not see without dropping by the corporate headquarters. Not all photos need to be serious; fun photos of events, people, and silly things hanging on the walls or found behind someone's desk can make someone want to do business with your company. The Boeing Airplanes account tweeted a link to a photo of the new 787 Dreamliner taking off from the Dallas Fort Worth airport.[11]

3. *Tweet a poll*—People like sharing their opinions, and they especially like doing it on Twitter. Post a simple poll using a Web-based tool like Twtpoll (twtpoll.com). It works like other items on Twitter where the link takes the user to a page to vote on the poll. A blog post can also contain an embedded poll, which drives traffic to your company site and provides a more controlled message. Polls can help guide future online messaging and marketing. Although the results of the poll can be shared using the functionality of the poll software, it can also be inspiration for a blog post. The poll results can also be shared on Twitter, or if they are more involved, you can share a link to the blog post with the results.

4. *Ask for volunteers*—Followers of your company are frequently willing to help out. Fans love to beta test products because it makes them feel important and on the inside. No matter what your product or service is, look for ways to get a small group of people to provide early insider feedback. Seek out these people on Twitter by asking for volunteers and asking likely candidates to participate. These customers

become brand advocates who promote company products and provide customer support to other prospects.

5. *Ask for product suggestions*—If customers feel connected to a company by making suggestions for marketing content and compelling offers to drive leads, they feel an even stronger connection by making product suggestions. Mobile phone company Nokia published a series of blog posts where interested people followed the design of a new phone and provided feedback each step of the way. Twitter updates can publicize this effort and give advocates the opportunity to share the new ideas. By supporting an initiative with a blog post, the links shared and spread on Twitter drive traffic back to the company site to pages with calls to action.

A simpler version of this is just asking for product suggestions on Twitter and asking users to submit them on the company website. This gives your company the opportunity to capture contact information as well as the product suggestions. Make sure to include an opt-in box to be in compliance with spam regulations before adding these individuals to an e-mail list.

Pushing the Twitter Envelope

If anyone thought that social media was all about hugs and "Kumbaya," they should take a look at Twitter's advertising program. It was launched to a small group of users, and one part of it is available to anyone. Users have the ability to promote an individual tweet, a trending topic, or even a Twitter account. Anyone can promote an account, but promoting tweets and topics are still in the beta stage.

When promoting a tweet, an advertiser selects a tweet that has already been published and indicates that the company would like to promote it. Now this tweet appears at the top of related search results and users can interact with it as if it is a normal tweet. The minimum monthly budget for any Twitter advertising program is $5,000, and the promoted tweets are based on cost per engagement (CPE). You are charged for every reply, retweet, click, and favorite of the tweet. The goal is to expose the tweet to more users than would normally see it and then have these viewers retweet it to their followers. This creates more possible impressions of the message and more clicks on the link included in the message.

A promoted trending topic allows an advertiser to pay for his or her keyword, which will be shown in the list of trending topics in the right sidebar of Twitter.com. When users click on the promoted trending topic, they are taken to the search results of that topic. American Express paid to promote their #SmallBizSat term to support their Small Business Saturday promotion. In mid-2011, promoted trending topics were rumored to cost $120,000 per day. Trending topics are frequently casual conversation starters, world events, and celebrity goings-on. B2B buyers are not used to looking at these topics for business information, so this is not a viable option for most B2B companies to reach their prospects.

The final advertising platform, and the one that seems to be the most successful, is the promoted account. Twitter has always been about whom to follow so users could see the most relevant information in their time-lines. When advertisers promote their Twitter accounts, they are shown in the "Who to Follow" section in the sidebar of Twitter.com. Promoted accounts are also shown to users who might be interested in the content, based on other accounts they follow. Gaining Twitter followers is about gaining both interested users and their reach. Paying to get both of these is an affordable way to share and spread a company message, especially when that message drives targeted traffic back to a website with clear calls to action. And when you know how many leads you can generate per fol-lower and what your cost per lead is, you can determine if paying to pro-mote your company Twitter account is a sound financial decision.

The other advantage of using the Twitter advertising platform is that it gives companies access to an analytics dashboard. This dashboard doesn't just monitor promoted tweets; it measures all tweets from the advertiser. This makes it possible for smart marketers to more fully track activity on Twitter and connect that activity to the sales funnel.

Twitter has been slow to add new features or functionality, but many common practices now incorporated in the platform were started by users and added by third-party developers. So even though it is a private com-pany, they do not entirely control how their users interact on the plat-form. Think of Twitter as a platform to provide information and education to those interested in your products and services. This is a trackable, tar-geted way to communicate in a place where your company has only so much control. Consistent use of Twitter will help you increase leads from social media sources.

Three B2B Twitter Steps
to Superstardom

1. *Create a Twitter content process*—Sharing great content is the best way to increase your Twitter reach. To share content, you need to identify industry resources that you can use as a content library. You should have 5 to 10 sources in this library so that you can follow the 10-4-1 rule of social sharing. Add them to Twitterfeed to automatically share articles from these industry thought leaders to your Twitter account. Create a Twitter list of prominent people in your industry to make it easy to retweet their updates. Start with a list of at least 100 Twitter users.

2. *Tweet landing pages*—Yes, you read that correctly. Share links to your landing pages on Twitter. Assuming you are taking our advice from step one above, the 10-4-1 rule mandates you tweet one landing page for every 10 thought-leadership articles you share. Make sure that the message that accompanies your landing page link is interesting and attention grabbing to maximize the number of followers who click your link.

3. *Test Twitter advertising*—Explore the self-service Twitter advertising interface and test using promoted accounts. If you already have a baseline number for how many leads you get per follower, calculate a cost per lead when you are paying for followers.

Maximizing Facebook Lead Generation through Engagement

Facebook is the largest social network on the planet, but you already know that. They are projecting how they are going to get to 1 billion users. As you read this they may already be there. If you work for a global business-to-business (B2B) company, this is especially relevant because a tremendous amount of their continued growth will be outside of the United States.

"With the sheer volume of active users on Facebook, there is absolutely a large portion of which that are businesspeople," said Mari Smith, one of the world's foremost experts on using Facebook as a marketing channel and coauthor of *Facebook Marketing: An Hour a Day.* "They are prime prospects for B2B companies. Though these businesspeople may predominantly use Facebook for personal reasons, they are still relatively easy to find with the data in their basic profile."

Before we continue to make the case for Facebook for B2B companies, realize that half of all Facebook users log on every day. If you can get your content in front of half a billion people daily, isn't that worth considering? Now let's see if your content is up to the challenge. We already know that content must be remarkable for people to take the first action, that is, to read or watch it.

Profiles versus Pages

Just to make sure you understand what part of Facebook we are talking about, it is the business Page. People have profiles and businesses have Pages. It is very easy to create a Facebook Page, but we will not detail the steps for doing it, as the Facebook interface can change. Go to www .facebook.com/business for the most current details on how to create your Page. The hard part of creating a Page is developing the content strategy to engage your fans, not building out the Page itself.

People who like a Facebook Page will be called fans in this chapter and throughout this book. Although they are no longer called fans on Facebook, it is just too cumbersome to call them "people who like your Page" and it's kind of creepy to call them likers. Most people still refer to them as fans, so we will do likewise.

It Made Sense for Cisco to Join

"While Cisco has had established Pages and Groups on Facebook for a couple years now, most of these pages are focused on one technology or business," Autumn Truong, manager of social media and corporate communications, told us in 2010. "In addition, there are Cisco Facebook Groups and fan Pages that aren't created by Cisco employees. We felt this was an opportunity for us to create a Facebook Page that is a 'one stop shop' for our community on Cisco news, events and information. Similar to how we have a corporate presence on our blogs and Twitter, we thought it was a great opportunity to have a similar presence on Facebook."[1]

Cisco now has one of the leading B2B company Facebook Pages with 200,000 fans that engage with the company's content at a high level.

Three Reasons to Create a B2B Presence on Facebook

1. *Search*—Search is a huge reason for B2B companies to have a presence on Facebook. Pages are public and accessible by search engines, so when prospects search for your products or services, you have the opportunity to show up in the search results. Once a Facebook Page gains 25 fans, you can select a custom name for the URL at www .facebook.com/username. Facebook.com/companyname is the most likely choice for the URL.

    Custom URLs, page names, and information on the Info tab should all be considered as part of search optimization on Facebook. Make sure links to your Facebook Page are included on your company website and links to your company website are included on your Facebook Page. Even though social recommendations are becoming a bigger part of search, links among your properties, in both directions, help Google understand the reach and influence of your business.

2. *Reach*—Reach is how far you can spread your content. As we talked about in Chapter 5, more reach is better than less reach. No matter how many prospects you have, the more people who can spread your content, the better off your company is. The average person has 130 Facebook friends. By posting compelling content on Facebook, you have the opportunity for that content to be shared and seen by someone you didn't even realize you were targeting.

3. *Content*—Content is the key to success on Facebook. When you post content that is larger than your products and your company, more people are likely to be interested. Social media pioneer Dell created a Facebook Page dedicated to sharing social media best practices for small businesses. This was content that was not related to buying or maintaining a computer, but something that anyone in business could relate to. Is there something unique in your industry that you can share on Facebook? Interview someone from human resources about changes in hiring practices and turn that into an ebook. If you keep things very general, it can be applicable to anyone in business.

Yes, Facebook Is for B2B

As much as people talk about the difference between B2B and business-to-consumer (B2C) marketing and the reasons why selling to another business is different than selling to a consumer, marketing superstars know that messages are directed at people at a company, not the company itself. Facebook is a collection of people and their interconnections with one another. As people log onto Facebook to check the latest updates from their friends, they are also looking for bite-size nuggets of information that can help them do their job better. Do people think they are going to Facebook for work information? Probably not, although they might tell their bosses they are.

But the reality of today's always-on work environment is that people are always thinking about work. They might not actively be looking for information about a new accounts payable computer module, but if your blog post about seven ways to eliminate paperwork in your accounting processes appears in the feed of an office manager, even at 10:30 at night, he or she will take notice. This click from Facebook needs to be as frictionless as possible. Users should be able to visit a mobile version of the blog and read it on their smartphones right when they see it or be able to e-mail it to themselves to read it the next morning.

"B2B companies are often guilty of posting always and only about themselves on Facebook: the awards they've won, the articles they've published, and the latest and greatest information about their latest and greatest product release," said Bryan Person, social media evangelist at LiveWorld. "The Page becomes little more than a glorified version of the company's corporate website. And while that approach may be helpful for the prospect who's researching the company for the first time, it won't generate enough likes and comments to regularly surface the content in the News Feed and help nudge fans through the buying cycle."

Now how can you make sure your content appears in the stream of her friends' update? There's an algorithm for that. It's called EdgeRank.

Understanding the EdgeRank Engagement Algorithm

The Facebook News Feed is the flow of updates and links from your friends and from Pages you like. This is what most people think of when they think of Facebook. The goal of a marketing superstar is to make sure your company's updates show up in a fan's News Feed if they are interested in your company. We have seen reports that as many as 95 percent of people who like your Page never return, which means that most people who read and interact with your content do so in their News Feed.

The way Facebook determines what shows up in a fan's News Feed is based on their EdgeRank algorithm. If you understand what influences EdgeRank, you can work toward helping your content show up more often. Every update, photo, and video is called an object. Once a fan interacts with the object, it gets an edge. The algorithm, which determines the rank of the edge is determined by three factors that have been made public: affinity, weight, and time. It is possible that other factors influence the EdgeRank too. It is possible that Facebook has changed the algorithm since it was introduced. And with how often Facebook engineers change their code, it is very likely.

Affinity is how an individual fan relates to your company's Page. If the person visits your Page or interacts with your content by liking it, commenting on it, or clicking on it, that person has a higher affinity for those updates or links your company posts. Comments rank higher than likes because it is a sign of greater engagement. This means that posted content will rank higher in the algorithm and Facebook will be more likely to show users your content in their News Feeds. You want to publish content that fans will interact with so that they see more of your company's content in the future. And this is a one-way relationship of the fan to the company, so no amount of the company liking the users' updates will influence the EdgeRank of what each individual fan sees.

Weight is determined by the type of content posted on your Page. Photos and videos have the most weight, followed by links, which are followed by status updates and likes. More engaging content is more likely to show up in the News Feed.

Time is also a factor in determining the EdgeRank of an object. Older content is less likely to show up in a fan's News Feed. You need to publish content at least once per day on your Facebook Page to make sure your fans will see an updated stream of content.[2]

10 Ways to Drive Leads on Facebook

Generating leads with content on Facebook is similar to generating leads on other platforms, but there are more opportunities to connect with prospects and customers. Marketers who understand what fans connect with are on the path to marketing superstardom. Facebook offers Page owners the opportunity to extend the brand experience on the site by creating additional custom tabs. The content for each tab is a Web page hosted elsewhere but displayed on Facebook. The benefit of this is that your tab can be completely custom and include Google Analytics or other tracking codes to help you accurately measure traffic from Facebook to your landing pages. These tabs are listed in the left-hand navigation, and each one has a unique URL; this means visitors can be directed to a particular tab from both inside and outside of Facebook.

Because of the number of opportunities on Facebook, it is a great place to experiment with different offers and calls to action. Try wording offers differently and track what works. Test an ebook title as a call to action. Compare that to posting a key point from the ebook.

1. *Welcome page for leads*—Not only can you direct visitors to a particular tab, but you can set one tab as the Page landing page or welcome page to visitors who have not liked the Page. That is the only category of visitors who can have the default landing page. Since we know that most people never return to the Page, it is imperative to get them to like the Page to even have a chance of seeing future updates. You will see lots of landing pages that have an arrow pointing to the like button or other ways of encouraging visitors to like the Page. This is called a Like Gate. Marketing firm ADG Creative had a simple message on their welcome tab, as seen in Figure 10.1. Step 1: Click "Like." Step 2: Be

FIGURE 10.1 ADG Creative Facebook Welcome Page

Heard. (www.facebook.com/ADGCreative). And they named the tab "Hi, we're your new agency," which showed in the navigation.

Liking a Page takes very little effort—only one mouse click—and it is not a true CTA, since there is no offer behind it. Some Pages do explain what the fan will get by liking the Page, but there is no exchange of information.

The Brainshark Page (www.facebook.com/BrainShark) features a video overview and a clear reminder to like the Page. But it also includes links to sign up for a free account and a link to test the cloud-based video presentation software.

It is different when there is an offer on the landing page that requires a sign-up form. This is your first opportunity to both connect with prospects and provide them content that will keep them engaged with your company moving forward.

2. *A landing page on Facebook*—If you have a particularly popular ebook or recorded webinar, create a version of the landing page sign-up form as a tab on Facebook. Remember that this tab has a unique URL, so you can drive people to this offer both from within Facebook and from outside of Facebook. This will let you understand how your prospects respond to the same offer on your website and on Facebook.

   Networking company Ciena offers a free acronym guide containing 30 pages of telecom acronyms when you like the Page.[3] They use a box with a Facebook Like button so that visitors have two buttons to click on to reveal the download page, as seen in Figure 10.2. They are not using this as a landing page for new visitors, nor are they trading this ebook for contact information. This is a missed opportunity for lead generation on Facebook.

3. *Newsletter sign up*—All marketing superstars have an e-mail newsletter, and we hope you are not the exception. Every outpost should have a sign-up form, or at least reminders to sign up for the e-mail newsletter. For the Facebook version, create a tab called "E-mail Sign Up." Post periodic reminders to the Wall, which will show in fans' News Feed, to sign up for the e-mail and include a link to the tab.

   E-mail provider MailChimp has a great newsletter sign-up page, which sets expectations for the regular e-mail and humorously strokes the ego of potential subscribers by claiming to only be for advanced users. "Power user? The MonkeyWrench is our sporadic newsletter chock-full of advanced MailChimp tips & tricks. We'll

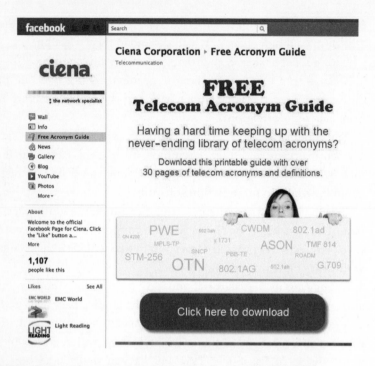

FIGURE 10.2 Ciena Corporation Facebook Landing Page

go over obscure features you never knew existed, how to hack stuff in MailChimp, and occasionally discuss advanced e-mail marketing concepts and best practices!"[4]

4. *Inclusion of content offers on the wall*—As we noted previously, when you publish content on the Page Wall, it shows up in fans' News Feeds. Yes, some people do visit your page and view your updates on the Wall, but they primarily view them in their News Feed, mixed in with updates from his former high school sweetheart and the hot girl from biology class who he never could work up the courage to ask out but friended her on Facebook anyway. There is a lot of emotional baggage wrapped up in the viewing of the News Feed, so updates like "Check out our latest blog post about purchasing downspouts" are never going to cut it.

If this is not an aha moment about the importance of the quality of your company's content, it should be. Facebook posts may not seem as fleeting as those posted on other social networks because they all live on your Page, but they still have to cut through the noise.

Develop your content according to an editorial calendar, but consider publishing it to different social media profiles at different times. Don't publish a blog post and automatically push it to Facebook, Twitter, and LinkedIn at the same time. Share them at different times, or even different days, with different headlines, to better your chance of reaching more people. Although there may be a concern that it may be too easy to miss manually publishing to Facebook, there is a benefit. If you automatically publish to Facebook using a third-party tool such as HootSuite or TweetDeck, it seems that sometimes Facebook is reducing the EdgeRank on those posts.

5. *The power of visual storytelling*—More photos are published on Facebook than on all other photo sites combined. Many of those photos depict late night exploits of your friends, not you . . . because marketing superstars know better than to post compromising pictures on the Internet, right? (Whether you have friended your boss on Facebook or not, your next boss might not be so enamored of your partying ways.)

   You should be posting photos on your company Page because it is a good way to tell a simple story. We have moved beyond company picnics and chief executive officer (CEO) award shots to show products in action, customer solutions, and behind-the-scenes views of your company.

   If a photo is good, short videos are better. Videos that you make to showcase your company solutions should be uploaded to YouTube so that they can be embedded on a blog, but they should also be uploaded to Facebook. Remember, the EdgeRank algorithm gives more weight to photos and videos, so uploading both directly to Facebook will improve the visibility of your other lead-generating content in your fans' News Feeds.

   SteelMaster Buildings, manufacturers of prefabricated structures, has uploaded numerous photos of custom-designed buildings in a variety of settings, as well as time-lapse videos to show how easy it is to install the buildings (www.facebook.com/SteelMasterBuildings).

6. *Social advertising*—Just like on other social media platforms, Facebook ads are worth considering. The benefit of Facebook ads is that they can be hypertargeted to your prospects and customers.

You can even target them to people who have already liked your Page to remind them about your remarkable content and compelling offers. Although social media provides you the ability to lower your cost per lead compared with traditional marketing efforts, even paid advertising on social media platforms has a lower cost per lead due to its ability to target more precisely based on demographics and stated interests.

Facebook estimates the target audience based on the details you select. This is another opportunity to get in front of likely leads. These ads generally appear on the righthand side of Facebook on various pages, so they compete in a different way for a visitor's attention. Facebook is responsible for nearly one-third of all online display ad impressions in the United States.[5]

After you work through the details of targeting, there is a budget section, which includes an amount to spend per day based on the amount Facebook estimates per click.

Since these are pay-per-click ads, you are charged only when users click your ads. Direct these ads to any tab on your Facebook Page or a destination outside of Facebook. Again it is relatively inexpensive to run a test to determine whether Facebook users are more likely to visit a Facebook destination or one on your company site or blog.

7. *Sponsored stories*—Another version of Facebook adverting is called Sponsored Stories, which automatically creates ads from a variety of actions by users. There are currently seven different actions that can generate Sponsored Stories that appear to friends of those taking action. They are Page Like, Page Post, Page Post Like, App Used, App Shared, Check-in and Domain.[6] We will only look at the ones most relevant to B2B companies on Facebook. The first is called a Page Like story. This is a simple ad that is displayed to people when one of their friends likes your company Page. But these ads can be targeted with all the demographics of Facebook ads. If you are just starting a Page, do not pay attention to this type of ad as you would not be targeting enough people.

There is another type called Page Post Like Story. This is also more effective when you have a larger number of Page fans because it shows people when one of their friends likes a post on your Page.

The type of Sponsored Story that works best for lead generation is the Page Post Story. These are ads that appear to fans of the Page every time you post an update on the wall. Although it is not known to affect the EdgeRank algorithm, this type of ad does give your fans another opportunity to be made aware of the content you are publishing and click on it. If your fans are used to seeing quality content from you, the ad is less intrusive and seen as a positive reminder. These inexpensive ads are a great way to test different methods of reaching your prospects.

A study by TBG that reviewed more than 4 billion ad impressions on Facebook found that by advertising to fans, companies could reduce the acquisition cost of registrations by 44 percent.[7]

8. *Giveaways*—Contests are huge on Facebook, but for a B2B company an irrelevant giveaway generates irrelevant leads. Companies have given away everything from T-shirts to books to vacations on Facebook, but think about what is useful for your prospects. Do you have a new product or service that you would like to promote? You can give away a free consultation that would normally be part of a sales process. Consider a higher level of customer support for existing customers.

The Facebook requirements for contests are very strict (www .facebook.com/promotions_guidelines.php), so be sure to review them carefully. The two biggest restrictions are that if you run a promotion on Facebook, it must be administered through a third-party app or a separate tab, and you cannot make a functional part of Facebook, for example liking a Page, commenting on a post, or uploading a photo, a requirement to enter the contest. As a marketing superstar, you can come up with something that is relevant to your business and drives relevant leads.

Create a contest that doesn't just live on Facebook but that can be promoted on multiple social media profiles.

9. *Livestreaming of Facebook with links*—Facebook provides the opportunity to add the Livestream app in a tab on your Page. This means you can easily broadcast a live, online video show to your fans from within Facebook. The Livestream software lets you shoot a live Web show that is broadcast to the Web, Facebook, and mobile devices all at the same time. When you create a Livestream channel

and display it on Facebook, previously recorded shows are available for watching too.

It should come as no surprise that we caution you not to start a live show on whim without a plan in place. If there is a huge event and you want to test the Livestream platform, go ahead and do it, but make real plans for how you are going to implement this into your ongoing plans.

Use this video platform to promote content that can drive leads for your B2B company. If you have an ebook with 10 ways to get more Facebook likes in your industry, discuss four or five of them on a show and let viewers know how they can download the ebook to get the rest of them. If the live show targets the right prospects, they will follow a link to learn more—and then become leads.

Network Solutions uses the Livestream app on their Facebook Page to create a small business channel, which features interviews and conference video. The video also includes a crawl at the bottom of the screen with a live link to download an ebook.[8]

10. *Referrals with incentive*—Your best customers may want to recommend you to their colleagues, or they may want to keep your solutions all to themselves. If your product provides a notable advantage in their business, they don't want to tell anyone—especially their competitors. But what about providing them an incentive to become a brand advocate. We're not talking about generating leads with a Starbucks or Amazon gift card. We are talking about offering customers something of value. Maybe it is access to a product engineer or the vice president of marketing. Maybe it is quicker customer support response time. Or maybe it is becoming part of a customer council. These are worth much more to customers than a cup of coffee, or even a mocha latte. Just like offers and contests need to make sense in the context of your business, so do incentives.

Facebook Engagement Means Leads

Your customers and prospects already log on to Facebook regularly. You also should be reminding them that your company has a presence there. Set the expectation that they are not just going to see the same posts on

LESSONS FROM A MARKETING SUPERSTAR

Name: Ekaterina Walter
Title: Social Media Strategist
Company: Intel Corporation
Years in Position: 2.5

What is your greatest social media/marketing success?
I believe the company reaches the greatest success when there is a widespread adoption and understanding of the importance of social media throughout the company. I cannot say that this is 100 percent true at Intel, but we are rather close. We have specific enablement efforts in place to enable our social media practitioners (SMPs) to be successful. We have an internal community for SMPs to stay in touch, we offer online as well as physical training worldwide, we create a monthly newsletter to keep them updated on the latest and greatest, we produce Point of View documents on the biggest changes/announcements in the industry.

On the campaign level I believe the ultimate success you can achieve is for your program to go viral. The greatest example is the Museum of Me application produced by Intel Asia and launched in May 2011. It went viral throughout the world and is now approaching 10 million views. The application that pulls in the data from your personal Facebook page and creates a story of your life truly resonated with people around the world and spread like wildfire. It is a testament of how a brand can connect with people on an emotional and personal level. That is what you want—to break through the clutter and touch hearts with your innovation.

What is your biggest roadblock in executing your social media strategy? The lack of the tools and analytics needed to truly measure your impact. The industry is fragmented, with hundreds of tools out there, each measuring just a fraction of what you need. To truly get the bigger picture and worldwide impact of your social programs, most of the time you

(continued)

(*continued*)

need multiple tools and manual analysis (which are both time-consuming and costly). There isn't one single tool that could measure your success on a strategic level and on a tactical/campaign level to show you your overall impact.

What is the single most important trait of a B2B marketer? The ability to sort through the clutter and not get distracted by the next shiny object. A lot of tools and communities that are suitable for B2C won't work very well for B2B marketing. You need to know your objectives, clearly set your strategy, and then build meaningful connections with your customers. Based on those, you need to identify which tools will get you to that ultimate goal and allow you to build those connections. Prioritizing your customers' needs is always a good idea—in any business.

Facebook that they see on Twitter or your blog. This is why marketing superstars create a global social media editorial calendar to organize what content is posted where and when.

"Make strategic use of the feature that allows posting on other business Page Walls and/or tagging as your business Page," offers Mari Smith. "This allows for tremendous networking and visibility for B2B companies. Don't try to market or sell through this technique; rather, simply seek to be of service, share valuable resources, and answer questions on other Page Walls where appropriate. Other businesses will see your company as one that is helpful and adds value and will feel more drawn to find out more about you."

Facebook provides the best opportunity for engagement with a community by posting a variety of content that fans will engage with. Remember the content with the highest weight in the EdgeRank algorithm? It is photos and videos. In the design of the EdgeRank system, Facebook programmers have told you that photos and videos get the most fan engagement by giving them the most weight. The more types of items you post that get engagement, the more engagement you get.

But what about calls to action?

And leads?

This is a two-step process of lead generation. Don't put on your dancing shoes yet. It's not that kind of two-step. The first step is to do everything you can to encourage engagement. Ask questions of your fans. Be real and have fun. Relate to holidays, current events, and happenings in your fans' world. Share links to blog posts, but encourage comments on your Facebook Page. Recent studies have shown that asking fans to like your updates increases the number of likes you get. That's no surprise, right? Ask and ye shall receive. And remember the affinity part of the EdgeRank algorithm? It is how each person connects with objects published by the Page and how much he or she engages with Page objects.

Creating more engagement early on will help your future updates—those containing compelling offers and calls to action—show up in fans' News Feeds. They can't click them if they don't see them. And they don't see them unless they click. That's why it's a two-step process.

Even though many people at B2B companies don't understand the intricacies of managing an effective Facebook Page, there are even fewer who can use them to drive leads. As you progress through this book, you are breathing rare air. You are more than halfway to becoming a marketing superstar.

Three B2B Social Media Facebook Steps to Superstardom

1. *Create a Facebook welcome page*—Set the expectation that new Facebook Page visitors should like your Page by creating a custom welcome tab. Once they like your Page, provide an opportunity for them to become a lead by including a form and offer directly on your Page. Examine the conversion rate for your Facebook landing page and compare it with those for landing pages on your website.

2. *Understand EdgeRank*—The Facebook EdgeRank algorithm is most likely to show photos and videos in fans' News Feeds versus other posted content. Rather than post images of the company picnic, post behind-the-scenes photos or videos that tell a story of the company—stories that are more compelling to your fans. Develop two stories

about your company that you can tell using images, with captions of course, and two more that you can tell using video.

3. *Test Sponsored Stories advertising*—Sponsored Stories that target existing fans of your Page have been found to be the most successful in lead generation. Create a 60-day test campaign of Page Post Sponsored Stories that shows fans the offers your company posts. Start with a small budget to understand if these ads can works for your B2B company. Use the hypertargeting of Facebook to segment your fans to determine which prospects are most likely to respond to which offers.

E-Mail Is Social

The average business e-mail user will send and receive 115 e-mails per day in 2012, predicts the Radicati Group.[1] Break through the crowded inbox of your prospects with compelling content.

Many people do not use separate e-mail boxes for business and personal purposes. For consumer companies, it means that they can reach their customers while they are busy with their job, but for business-to-business (B2B) companies, this means that they can reach their customers during off-hours, when less is happening—times like early mornings, nights, and weekends. According to data gathered by social media scientist Dan Zarrella, e-mail sent between 6 AM and 7 AM has the highest click-through rate.[2]

Why would you want to communicate with your prospects in the morning? They are less distracted and more able to focus on the e-mail. By sending remarkable offers to them at this time, they will click to learn more. Ignore the myth of Tuesday at 11 AM as the best time to send customer e-mails, and test various send times to determine the best time for your prospects and customers.

Opt-In Is a Better Call to Action

In previous sections of this book we have provided ways to connect with prospects to get them to raise their hands to express interest in your company's product. We all understand the top of the funnel applications of lead generation. This is what you did before social media. Create offers and drive prospects to those offers by whatever means necessary. Social media and content marketing have provided marketers with more ways to drive people to those offers. The offers can also be more targeted than the broad strokes of traditional media.

But e-mail can be a better path to marketing superstardom. An e-mail sign-up is a common call to action (CTA) for B2B marketers and frequently has less friction than 10 fields on a landing page form. A prospect will opt-in to an e-mail newsletter without reservations, especially if you set the expectations of what they will receive with what frequency. For example, sign up for our e-mail newsletter to receive a new tip each week to optimize your logistics business.

This tells subscribers that they will receive a simple e-mail each week with a tip. The magic in this relationship is that from one simple sign-up, you have received permission to contact these customers or prospects each week, providing you keep up your end of the bargain. This gives you the opportunity to move prospects further along the buying process with subsequent offers.

In the previous example, let's say there are 10 weekly e-mails, each providing one tip. Once you get to tip number eight, start laying the groundwork for what comes next. These tips have provided prospects with valuable information to help them in their current situations. What does it take to move them to the consideration phase of the process. This may be controlled by outside forces, such as budget and an already established timeline, but provide an additional offer that they can respond to. This could be something as simple as an ebook of the 10 tips they already received with 5 bonus tips. More information would be required to sign up for the ebook, but they already know the value of the information and would willingly trade more contact data for it. Once they fill out the form, they become leads.

Other methods of lead generation require marketers to continue to earn the trust of their audience each and every time. Every offer must be compelling. Every piece of content must be remarkable. Every CTA must be clearly communicated to encourage action. But the e-mail opt-in is a one and done.

E-mail opt-ins should not exist in only one place. A CTA for e-mail sign-up should be on a website and on a blog. The offer for repeated content via regular e-mail can be shared in updates on social networks such as Twitter and LinkedIn. These should be posted with the same frequency as the e-mail. For example, remind your Twitter followers once a month about your monthly e-mail newsletter. Plus post a link to it every time you publish a newsletter. Facebook gives marketers the opportunity to embed a sign-up form in a unique tab. This means updates on Facebook encouraging fans to sign-up for an e-mail do not have to leave the Facebook environment to do so.

Why Nobody Likes E-Mail

Everyone receives more e-mail than they can manage, and sometimes any targeted business e-mail is lumped in with the spam e-mail that makes it through our myriad of filters. Can you believe that approximately 89 percent of all e-mails are spam, resulting in an estimated 260 billion spam e-mails sent every single day?[3] Many people forget they subscribe to e-mails when they receive them and relegate them to their spam folders, never to see e-mails from that source again.

Our goal as marketers is to make e-mails so enticing that our prospects can't wait to click on each one to see what we have to offer. And they can't wait for the next e-mail. A B2B company that becomes known for the irreverent tone in their e-mails, so long as they are providing valuable information. is doing something right. Although you may not be the target customer, ask yourself if the subject line is enticing enough to click and read more? Although social media is not about interruption, as is much of traditional marketing, the first step of e-mail is.

People wade through e-mails all day long, trying to delete as many as they can. No matter what type of approach they take to get things done, an e-mail saved for later often gets pushed too far down in the inbox. The goal is to get a prospect to read a message immediately and take action now. Creating urgency in e-mail is key!

12 Ways to Get More Leads Out of E-Mail

1. *Do I know you?*—Make e-mails more personal by choosing a sender's name that people recognize, instead of your company name. This could be the chief executive officer (CEO), the head of sales or marketing, or another notable person from your company. People are more likely to open an e-mail from a person, especially a person whose name they are familiar with.

2. *What's it all about?*—Use the subject line to set expectations for recipients. Let them know the contents of the e-mail before they open it. Don't say things like "Our Company's Weekly Update or Monthly E-Mail Newsletter." Be specific with subjects such as "Five Ways to Grow Your Insurance Business" or "Report from Global Communications World 2012."

3. *Offer them the world*—The most successful lead generation e-mails present one compelling offer, a clear CTA, and expectations of what's on the other side of the click. This is called a dedicated send and can be sent to a segmented list of prospects or customers based on data of what they are interested in.

4. *The mouse has landed*—Every click on an e-mail offer needs to take prospects to a clear landing page. These should be optimized so that visitors know exactly what to do when they arrive. If they clicked on an offer to receive an ebook, they should come to a page that tells them what to do to get that ebook—and nothing else. Subsequent offers for related ebooks can be offered on a thank-you page or in a follow-up e-mail.

5. *All links rise with the tide*—The behavior of people does not always match our expectations. Most would think that the click-through rate for any individual link would be higher if there were fewer links. There is less likely to be confusion on the part of the viewers, and they would click on the most obvious links in an expected number. Social media scientist Dan Zarrella conducted an e-mail study and found that the more links that were contained in an e-mail, the higher the click-through rate of all links.[4]

6. *Put down what you want to hear*—E-mails must be relevant to subscribers or the best subject lines, offers, and calls to action will be wasted. Don't send e-mail simply to keep regular communication going. Create an ongoing plan of relevant content-based offers that will drive leads. If you have a steady flow of content on the company blog, consider compiling that into an ebook with the addition of an introduction from an outside industry expert. This adds new context to information your prospects may have already seen.

7. *You talking to me?*—Any standard e-mail program allows you to segment your sends to appropriate members of your audience. Although an e-mail opt-in allows you to continue to contact subscribers without them taking additional action, if you provide information that does not relate to them, they will unsubscribe. If a prospect is interested in products from your health care division, he or she is not likely interested in seeing offers from your aviation division. Your results per e-mail will be higher if you send e-mails to only relevant prospects.

8. *Nurture leads throughout the buying cycle*—An initial e-mail opt-in is a top of the funnel action. A prospect is interested in your

products or services and wants to learn more. That person also might be exploring how you deal with prospects. Once he or she has received a variety of information and has demonstrated movement along in the buying cycle, that prospect needs to be considered part of a different segment. The prospect is not a lead until he or she fills out an offer form. Once crossing over to lead status, these leads need to be nurtured, not pitched. Content offers need to be more specific to your solutions for their industry. This is where having information about all their interactions and downloads is critical; it allows you to understand what they need next. They should no longer be receiving e-mails from a marketing vice president, but from the salesperson who has or will help in the next stages of the buying cycle.

9. *Test, test, test*—One of the best things about digital marketing is the ability to test elements of an offer and review which one has better results. This makes your next campaign even better. The most important thing to test with an e-mail is a subject line. This determines whether recipients open the e-mail or not. Test different offers and calls to action. A trial software offer may not be right for new subscribers, but they might be interested in a white paper on managing customer expectations. Make sure the wording you are testing is extremely different. Subtle differences do not yield widely different results.

10. *Evaluate plain vanilla text e-mails versus the chocolate of HTML*— Most e-mail programs can receive an HTML, or designed, e-mail and do not require plain text e-mail. But many programs have images turned off by default. This means that an e-mail that is one big image may look blank to subscribers. And with the increasing use of mobile devices, there is a revived interest in creating and sending a plain text e-mail along with an HTML e-mail. Run a series of test sends to determine whether plain text e-mails are required by your audience. If your target is a highly technical audience, or engineers, they might prefer a lightweight text e-mail.

If you are still in the planning stages and have not yet sent lead-generating e-mails, review the analytics from your website as a proxy for your potential e-mail subscribers. Look at operating systems and devices to determine the prevalence of mobile devices among your target audience. And eat some ice cream while you are reviewing the stats. We would naturally choose chocolate.

11. *Everyone is reading e-mail on the go*—In the next chapter we will talk more about the mobile implications that should be taken into account for all your marketing efforts, but for this chapter we will address e-mail only. According to a Forbes study, 82 percent of executives have smartphones.[5] And 64 percent of decision makers check their e-mail on their phones.[6] Have you looked at the e-mails you send on a mobile device? Are your offers clear? Do recipients know what to click on? Smartphones can display HTML e-mails, but everything is small. Optimize these e-mails for mobile devices. Some mobile operating systems enlarge e-mails to make them easier to read. Learn which ones these are. Also, view the landing pages on these devices so that you can know what your prospects are seeing.

    Everyone's focus is on smartphones, but what do you do with an audience who still uses feature phones? If they receive e-mail on their phones, it is only text-based and their mobile browser ability is limited. This is another instance of knowing your audience to determine the best type of e-mails and landing pages to increase your number of leads.

12. *How often is too often?*—Just as more links drive more traffic through all links—not less—more frequent e-mails, of relevant, quality offers and content, provide more engagement. In early 2011, MarketingProfs, the marketing content, education and events company, changed their weekly e-mail to a daily e-mail. According to Ann Handley, chief content officer, based on site traffic and other engagement metrics, "The audience is more engaged with MarketingProfs, not less. The design of the e-mail is created to be short, quick, easy to ingest. It is very scannable, so recipients know what to expect and find out quickly if there is something for them."

Testing E-Mail Ideas Using Social Media

Testing is an important part of any marketing campaign, and social media provides a great testing ground to test aspects of your e-mail campaigns before you click Send. Testing your offers on your social media profiles is a good way to see how they resonate with your prospects.

Say you have determined that people who like your Facebook Page are more likely to be existing customers than casual fans or prospects.

Develop an offer for those customers. Create a Facebook landing page for the offer, and share that offer in different status updates on different days. You can do this a couple of times to generate some data about which offer is preferred. The preferred offer is the one that should be sent in an e-mail to existing customers.

Want to do some pretesting on an e-mail subject line? Send the options out as tweets first. Try to hold as many things constant as possible to make the test valid. Do not change the offer; change only how you describe it and its relevance to your target audience. Remember to make the tweets very different, rather than testing subtle word changes. For example, let's say we are testing a health care consultant firm's offer for an ebook called "Seven Steps to Six Sigma Mastery." On Tuesday, tweet "Master Six Sigma Now! Download our free guide now" with a trackable link. On Wednesday, tweet "Free ebook: 'Seven Steps to Six Sigma Mastery'" with a trackable link. Make sure you review click-throughs and conversion rates to determine which will be a better subject line for an e-mail about the ebook.

E-mail design can also be tested online before sending live offers. Create two layouts that show the calls to action but not the offer itself. Submit this to ABtests.com to receive feedback on the design from others outside of your target audience. Share the link on your company profiles to allow your network to provide feedback as well.

Four Ways to Socialize a Prospect's Inbox

E-mail is still the most pervasive communication tool and has even replaced the telephone for some people. Businesspeople live in their inboxes. This includes your boss, your colleagues, your customers, and your prospects. There are many ways to bring a social experience to a prospect's inbox; we will look at four of them.

1. *Connect on social networks*—The first and most obvious is to include social media profile links in your outgoing e-mail. Prospects need to know that there are multiple ways to connect to your company, and the repetition of seeing the Twitter, Facebook, and LinkedIn icons in the e-mail sidebar will help. It has been shown that it is not enough to show just the logo; add the words "Follow us on Twitter and show the URL if possible." It also helps set expectations and let

prospects know what to expect on each platform. This is why it is important to have a unique approach to each.

2. *Share on social networks*—When prospects receive a compelling offer, their initial inclination is not to share this with their network. But the first thing to make that happen is to make it easy. If the offer is to watch a webinar, make sure the webinar includes Share buttons to share with their networks. Although they might not want to share such a resource with their competitors, they would certainly want to gain the karma of sharing something of value with their networks.

3. *Include e-mail Share buttons on blog posts*—It is very common to see Share on Twitter buttons on blog posts, but what about Share via e-mail buttons? When you create blog posts that address the issues your prospects face in their businesses every day, they are going to want to share them with their colleagues. E-mail is how they want to do that.

4. *Include e-mail Share buttons in ebooks*—As we talked about in Chapter 6, one of the best offers to drive leads is a compelling ebook. All content you produce should include Share buttons so that prospects can share it with their networks. One button that is frequently overlooked is the share via e-mail. This is critical for prospects, because they are generally inclined to share elements from an ebook or the entire ebook with their internal team. Although they may be able to share this over an internal network, the way to facilitate internal sharing from within the ebook is an e-mail link.

Social Profiles within the Inbox

If you use Outlook for your corporate e-mail, as many do, LinkedIn provides a way to literally socialize your inbox. With the addition of this plug-in (www.linkedin.com/outlook), e-mails from your connections show information from LinkedIn. A separate folder shows all LinkedIn connections with most recent updates and things that they have shared. And if you receive an e-mail from someone who is not a LinkedIn connection, you can request the connection right from that e-mail.

If you use Gmail for corporate e-mail, Rapportive (www.rapportive .com) does the same thing for an inbox, but it includes other social media profiles besides LinkedIn. These are two ways that your inbox can easily help you expand your reach on your social networks by allowing you to connect with people you already communicate with.

E-mail is one of the most effective marketing tactics for B2B marketers to connect with prospects regularly and to share compelling offers to drive lead generation. Its effectiveness improves when it also leverages a company's social media presence for both content and reach. Marketing superstars know how to maximize the results from this approach.

Three B2B Social Media E-Mail Steps to Superstardom

1. *Create e-mails that people like*—With all the incoming messages prospects receive every day, it is imperative that the e-mail subject lines communicate the compelling content that you have sent. Once you have selected the offers to include in the e-mails, craft subject lines that describe the content. For subject line ideas, review successful blog post titles about similar content. You could even consider a small Google AdWords or Facebook ad campaign to test response rates to subject lines.

2. *Nurture leads*—E-mail isn't only for lead generation. E-mail can also shorten the buying cycle. Use your e-mail service provider or marketing automation software to schedule a series of targeted e-mail messages that are automatically sent to leads over a given period of time to help further address the problems they were working to solve when they filled out their first landing page.

3. *Test! Test! Test!*—For many marketers, e-mail is the largest driver of online leads. Because of this it is critical to ensure that e-mail marketing campaigns are as effective as possible. Begin testing important components of your e-mail marketing, such as subject lines, call-to-action placement, and time of day sent. Establish three variables of your e-mail marketing messages to test. Over 90 days, conduct tests using portions of your e-mail list to determine e-mail best practices specific to your prospects and leads.

PART

III

Taking Social Media Lead Generation to the Next Level

Stop Preparing for the Mobile Web; It's Here

Irfan Khan, vice president and chief technology officer (CTO) of Sybase, described the emerging benefits of mobile technology on CIO.com as: "improved customer engagement, unparalleled customer service, improved supply chain operations and partner/supplier collaboration as well as faster, more effective business decision-making."[1]

New studies trumpeting the fact that mobile phone usage is overtaking the PC are continually released. Even executive chairman of Google, Eric Schmidt, has said that mobile phone use is growing faster than his company's internal predictions. A 2010 Gartner report predicted that the total number of mobile phones with browsers that can access the Web will exceed the total number of PCs by 2013.[2]

This is information based on worldwide trends, but what if you look at this related to your business. If you are on track to becoming a marketing superstar, we can assume you have a mobile phone. Doesn't everyone you encounter have a mobile phone? But we are talking about smartphones specifically. You have one of those, right? Of U.S. consumers, 36 percent have smartphones.[3] And 82 percent of executives have smartphones.[4] Your buyers are spending more time checking e-mail, searching for business information, and logging on to social networks on their smartphones each day.

Getting Smart about Smartphones

We have spent most of this book writing about remarkable content driving leads and influencing business outcomes. You might have assumed that all this content was being consumed on a desktop. However, your customers are using mobile devices to check Twitter and Facebook. That link to your blog post needs to go to a mobile-optimized version of your company blog. And that carefully designed e-mail? How does it look on a mobile device?

Even if prospects can zoom in to find a link to click in the e-mail, what does the landing page look like when they get there? We will look at mobile landing pages shortly, but for now, keep all this in mind as we look at mobile content.

As we write this, Apple's mobile operating system, iOS, continues to grow in corporate environments with the sales of iPhones and iPads. Phones running the Android open-source operating system from Google are expanding market share with consumers, but many corporate information technology (IT) departments are concerned about security on the easily modified device. What has happened to the BlackBerry, the smartphone of choice for the corporate road warrior? It has suffered from a lack of support by app developers, which means that it has not been easy for users to customize their smartphone experience beyond the core functions of the phone (cell phone, calendar, e-mail, and Web browsing).

The percentage of U.S. smartphone subscribers who owned a BlackBerry device in May 2011 was 25 percent, down from 42 percent a year earlier.[5] We expect this number to have continued to drop by the time you read this.

If you, or anyone you know, currently has a BlackBerry running on a corporate network, it is likely that your next phone will be an iPhone. More than half of BlackBerry owners have indicated that they will switch to an iPhone upon its latest release.[6] That's right; the iPhone has buttoned up and gone corporate. That doesn't mean you can't nestle it in a sparkly case or one emblazoned with your favorite X-Man. That's Wolverine in our case.

When you view your website on a smartphone, what does it look like? If you have made no provisions for mobile, it appears like a toy website and visitors have to zoom in and scroll around to find what they are looking for. Even the best-designed site for a computer screen does not look good in this mode. Some coded functions won't work at all. If Adobe Flash has been used for menus or a rotating hero image, stop reading this book right now and eliminate all use of Flash. That will not show up on an iPhone or iPad and is not ideal for search engine optimization.

To be a true marketing superstar in the digital age, you must understand some of the common terms of programming and technology. Look at your

Web analytics to see what kind of mobile devices people use to visit your company website. If the iPhone or iPad dominates the mobile traffic, you need to be able to confidently tell your Web developers to replace the Flash elements with JavaScript or HTML5 so that visitors can view the site.

Two Ways to Mobile-Optimize a Website

"Without optimizing for the mobile environment," says Christina "CK" Kerley, business-to-business (B2B) marketing specialist, in her ebook, *The Mobile Revolution and B2B* (B2BMobileRevolution.com), "your site is creating an unusable, illegible experience on the one device that is always on and always within your target audiences' reach. Wide-ranging mobile tools and cool apps aside, your first step is to optimize your existing content."

There are two primary ways to mobile-optimize your company website, and there is one good reason to do it: mobile search engine optimization (SEO). It probably would not surprise you that the factors that determine which websites come up in mobile search are different than the factors responsible for optimization on the desktop Web. Location is a big part of mobile SEO because the algorithm knows it is a mobile phone. Mobile means the phone can move. It is not quaintly wired to the wall, like a wired phone or desktop computer.

According to Marissa Mayer, Google's vice president of local, maps, and location services, 20 percent of all searches are local and it's even higher on mobile devices. It's about 40 percent of mobile search.[7]

One important factor to determine which pages return in your mobile search results is how each page renders on your mobile devices. A nonoptimized site does not display well on most mobile devices, so that counts against it in future mobile searches. How you choose to optimize your site and landing pages for mobile makes a difference too.

A style sheet is a separate document that tells Web browsers how to display all elements of a website. This allows programmers to easily change the look of a site by changing the code once, instead of having to change it on every page across the site. The best way to understand the power of CSS, or cascading style sheets, is to go to cssZenGarden.com.

Choosing a different style sheet completely changes how the same content is displayed.

1. *Create a mobile style sheet*—A mobile-specific style sheet called handheld.css (and a second one called iphone.css) indicates to a mobile browser how to display all the content of your company website. The advantage of this method is that the existing site content can be used, rather than creating duplicate content. This method takes advantage of existing SEO work that has been done on the site. Things like title tags and keyword-optimized copy don't have to be recreated. The mobile style sheets can even indicate which content loads, thereby creating a mobile version of your original site.

2. *Create a separate mobile site*—Many marketers do not understand the power of CSS and think they need to build a second site. One site is preferable, but there may be technical limitations that force you to build a second, mobile-only site. If you must, make sure the site is located at mycompany.com/mobile. This way you can still take advantage of SEO of your main site, but your content will be duplicated in the subdirectory.

   The main site should have an automatic mobile detection code installed; this way, when a mobile device accesses the site, the user is redirected to the mobile site. If you are not able to install this redirect, add a link for visitors to click to view the mobile site.

Rand Fishkin, chief executive officer (CEO) and cofounder at SEOmoz.org, advises that there is little need for a separate mobile site. "Mobile copies of websites seem to me to be more likely to cause duplicate content issues, technical challenges, waste engineering resources and draw away attention from real mobile opportunities than to earn slightly higher rankings in mobile searches. Until/unless things change dramatically, I can't, in good conscience, recommend this practice (unless your regular site is absolutely unusable on a mobile device)."[8]

No matter which method you choose, you need to look at it from a lead generation standpoint. Make sure that your offers are clear and the calls to action are obvious. View the site on multiple mobile devices while it is in development to ensure everything works the way you expect it to. See what it is like to fill out the lead form on a smartphone. Will prospects do what you are asking in exchange for what you are offering, or will they pack up and walk right out the door? They are already mobile, after all.

On the Go with Mobile Content

So what does mobile content look like? Start by viewing your regular content. You are creating content that your prospects want to use to solve their problems, not content that is focused on products and features. Your content has to be so valuable that prospects are willing to trade for it. Not baseball cards or marbles, but something more valuable—their contact information. How willing are you to part with yours? Maybe you have a superstrong spam filter, and you can happily give out your e-mail address. Maybe you have a capable assistant who screens all of your phone calls. Its name is voice mail.

But does this describe your target audience? If your B2B company produces products that require delivery in a tractor trailer and a team of PhDs to prepare the documentation, the ultimate decision maker may be the chief information officer (CIO) or a vice president. These people don't give up their contact information easily. Now you know why junior people are the ones who research products. They don't know any better than to trade their e-mail address for your ebook.

But before we talk about mobile content that can generate leads, let's look at some basic content ideas that can drive traffic, namely, your company website and your company blog. As business executives spend more time on their mobile phones, whether out and about or sitting in a meeting in their office, they can arrive at your site by one of three ways.

The first is through mobile search. They are looking for a product or a solution to a problem, and their mobile search engine returns your site or a specific blog post. The second is based on information you share on social networks and through e-mail. The third is from recommendations from their network. In all these cases, the page they land on should be optimized for mobile display and relevant for mobile consumption.

You need to understand your customer funnel so that you can present the right kinds of information that customers or prospects will read on their mobile devices. If you sell products that require a Material Safety Data Sheet (MSDS), it probably is not reasonable for users to read it on their smartphones, but it would be great to let them know it is available. It is also helpful to give people the ability to easily e-mail it to themselves, and others, for later review. But an engineer on the factory floor who needs to check the data before proceeding still might want to look at all that tiny type on his or her phone. Usually these files are PDFs, which are easily viewable in a variety of mobile apps, such as iBooks on an iPhone.

The fastest-growing segment of time spent on mobile phones is that spent on social networking. According to Edison Research, 64 percent of regular social network users have posted updates to one or more social networks from their mobile phone.[9] This means that content your company promotes on its social media profiles needs to point to mobile-optimized content. If you think your B2B company is behind on adopting social media, you are probably even further behind in adopting mobile. But if you have even begun thinking about how to incorporate mobile optimization into your marketing strategies, then you are already ahead of the curve. For some reason, even though all marketers have a mobile phone in their pocket, many have a blind spot when it comes to adequately planning for the importance of mobile in their marketing mix.

A company blog needs a mobile view, whether added through a total site mobile style sheet or with a mobile-friendly plug-in. If you are running a WordPress blog, WPtouch[10] is a popular plug-in that restyles your blog to be friendly for touchscreen mobile devices (iPhone, Android, and some BlackBerries). This plug-in optimizes type size and renders the blog for the width of the mobile screen. No zoom and scroll is required on the part of your visitors reading your blog posts.

Many blogs feature calls to action in their sidebar. "Learn more about our product." "Let us contact you." "Sign up for a product demo." But in a mobile-optimized blog this sidebar is not shown because the text in the main column is rendered across the whole screen. This is why you need a CTA in every blog post. You want to make sure your offers are seen. If you use a plug-in to mobilize your content, make sure you understand what parts your blog show up on a mobile device. Check your blog on multiple devices to see how it is rendered on each.

Make sure you check it every time you add a new plug-in or update existing plug-ins. The disadvantage of using an open-source system of plug-ins such as WordPress is that there is no coordination between third-party developers. There is no one looking at the big picture or making sure the most common set of plug-ins work together when updates happen. Unfortunately that is the job of a marketing superstar.

What Is the Context of Your Content?

The reason they are called mobile phones is because you take them with you. Think back to this morning when you were on your way to the office. You walked down the street and almost got hit by a passing bus. You looked down to find yourself standing in a puddle.

You made a quick stop in the local coffee shop for what used to be called a large coffee. It is now called something you are not quite sure how to pronounce. You made it to the office and went straight to the conference room for a meeting. In the middle of the meeting you needed to look up some information for a new project that you will need in your next meeting.

Your morning is very similar to your prospects. This is the context of compelling mobile content. One way to think about context is to consider when and where someone needs the information. But we need to think more about the environment in which someone is consuming information on his or her mobile phone. It is frequently one where the user is either multitasking or on the go, with many other things competing for attention. Can you compete with a bus almost running someone down? If you can't, you may want to rethink the content you are producing.

Rethinking the Mobile Landing Page

In Chapter 2 we talked about the simplicity of landing pages and removing friction for visitors so that they take the required action. This approach is even more critical on a mobile landing page. You created a compelling mobile offer and a prospect clicked on it. That person might be riding on a train, waiting in line for coffee, or even walking down the street. Now you are asking him or her to fill out a form.

Ask prospects for the minimum amount of information required. Limit the number of open text fields and use radio buttons or drop-down menus for the prequalifying fields to make it easier to complete the form. When someone is already in a distracted environment, the last thing you want to do is make the form so difficult that the user doesn't complete it.

A mobile landing page needs to be designed with the space and slower download speeds in mind. See an example in Figure 12.1. The

FIGURE 12.1 Example of Mobile Landing Page

real estate of the screen is much smaller than a desktop and you don't want users to have to zoom in to read field label and zoom out to enter data.

If your company website serves up a mobile landing page, then all of the subsequent functions need to be based on mobile phone use. A prospect might download and read an ebook on the smartphone or view a video, but it depends on where that person is. Upon completion of the form, return a thank-you page that acknowledges that the user is on a mobile phone and let him or her know you have e-mailed a link with the requested content. This way, the user can choose to view the material on the phone or wait until they are back at the office.

Your goal is to make sure prospects can easily complete this transaction on their mobile phones, so a tracking file, or cookie, can be saved to their mobile browser. This is for better tracking and future identification. This isn't scary; it's the way the Internet works. That's how Amazon recognizes you when you come back to the site. It's the same technology.

B2B Mobile Apps Are for Suckers

It is a curious paradox that the availability of mobile apps is the thing that drove the explosive growth of the iPhone and Android-based phones, as well as what drove sales of BlackBerries into a tailspin, but their ongoing effectiveness for B2B marketing and lead generation is limited.

Hundreds of thousands of apps are available for a variety of platforms. The average iPhone user in the United States has downloaded 48 apps to his or her phone, and Android users have an average of 35. Not surprisingly, BlackBerry users lag behind, with an average of 15 apps on their phones. And of those who have downloaded apps, 68 percent of iPhone users use their apps multiple times per day, compared with 60 percent of Android users and 45 percent for BlackBerry users.[11]

These apps extend the functionality of a smartphone, but most apps are downloaded, used once, and never used again. So what about the ones created as marketing vehicles for B2B companies? Compelling? Nope. Remarkable? Not likely. And what value do they offer to users? Again, not much.

In March 2011, 100 million iPhone apps were downloaded and 81 percent of them were free.[12] Although smartphone users are more likely to abandon free apps, it also happens with the ones they have paid for with their hard-earned latte money.

We reviewed a variety of iPhone apps for B2B companies, and the ones that seem to be the most effective are the ones that extend the enterprise computing environment to a mobile device. Examples of these are apps by Salesforce.com and Oracle that allow users of existing software to review and enter data that lives on a network server or in the cloud.

These are contrasted with numerous apps from marketing firms and publications that include blog and Twitter feeds within the app and not much more. Why would someone want to go to a special app just to read a company's Twitter feed? Some of these apps even showed a mobile-friendly summary of a post, only to load the regular Web page, complete with small type, sidebars, and ads. The arrogance of these apps is pretty mind-boggling. Are your social streams so interesting that we want to go to a special app to read just them? And only them? Compelling content spreads and is shared by members of a company's network so that additional people discover it. Sequestering it in your own app does not help spread your content.

The best B2B app is a location-based sales tool that we will discuss in the next section. Other general apps that help salespeople manage their jobs, such as time trackers, receipt catalogers, and industry-specific news aggregators, extend the function of the smartphone and are worthwhile apps for B2B company employees.

It is also technology that is driving the change away from apps. HTML5 is a mobile-friendly version of the language many Web pages are written in. The flexibility of mobile websites is pushing developers to extend the experience of the mobile Web, rather than hiding value and functionality of their ideas in a walled application. Creating a mobile Web application in this manner means developers have to build it only one time, rather than rewriting it for each popular mobile platform. These days, apps are usually built for iPhones or Android first, and rarely for BlackBerry.

So, as a B2B marketer, what kinds of mobile apps should you explore producing. First, think about an app that runs on the mobile Web, rather than something to be downloaded to someone's phone. You need to ask the value question. What is something that will provide enough value to your customers or prospects? And it needs to connect to your business. Although you may be asking them to pay with their contact information (we are trying to generate leads, remember?), would customers pay money for it? If you are offering a free app, the best way to evaluate how compelling it is, is to ask if anyone would pay to use it and if there is a business context where it makes sense.

iPads and other tablets continue to explode on the scene, so this is a whole other category where you will get internal requests for tablet apps. Do not invest your marketing budget in these projects without understanding the value of their development and how it drives leads and business. You are on your way to becoming a marketing superstar, and you need to stand firm. Don't buckle under the pressure to build a shiny object app.

Location Is for Sales, Not Marketing

One part of the mobile ecosystem that we have not talked much about is location. That's because location is far more relevant to the B2B sales function. Although there have been plenty of location-based promotions around trade shows and other events, B2B companies have seen limited success driving on traffic and awareness with mobile check-ins Foursquare. The pool to draw from is quite small because according to Edison Research, only 4 percent of American's have ever checked in.[13]

We mentioned previously that the best B2B mobile app was a sales tool and it was created by Hoover's, a company that provides insight and analysis about companies to be used in a sales context. Once you download the app to your phone, it uses your current location and shows you companies nearby. In this app, which is available free to anyone, including Hoover's nonsubscribers, you can see company contact information, industry, annual sales, and key people in the company. You can view the companies in a map or list view, sort by size, and filter by industry. Salespeople can find new prospects on the fly if they have time to spare between appointments.

As with many things in this book, mobile marketing is something that some B2B companies are already doing well, but most have not quite wrapped their heads around how much it changes their approach to marketing. Your prospects will only be spending more time on their mobile devices in the future, not less. If you want to be part of their plans, you need to be there with them.

"Instead of a society that looks ahead, we are now a culture that constantly (and literally) looks down—because the amount of activity in our days, and the opportunities for our businesses, is depicted by the levels of activity occurring on our mobile screens," says Christina "CK" Kerley. "Put another way: the data that we send, store, and receive on our smartphones is always viewed as a priority."

Three B2B Social Media Mobile Marketing Steps to Superstardom

1. *Prioritize mobile*—Quality mobile traffic continues to grow as more decision makers spend more time seeking out information on their mobile phones. Review your Google Analytics or other Web analytics to determine how much of your current traffic is coming from mobile devices. This information will help you prioritize mobile in your existing marketing budget. Once 5 to 10 percent of your website traffic is mobile, it is time to consider elevating it in the budget.

2. *Discover the most popular mobile content*—Check your site analytics for the 10 most popular pages on your website in the past

12 months. Look at the 10 most popular pages on mobile. Look at both of these stats for the past month to see if it has changed. Continue to do this monthly for the next six months to spot any trends as you develop your mobile strategies.

3. *View your site on different devices*—Different mobile devices display Web pages differently. View your company website and company blog on the three most common smartphones (iPhone, Android, and BlackBerry) and two different tablets (iPad and one other), or use a mobile emulator such as Litmus (Litmus.com). Use the list of your site's most visited pages from step 2 and make note of the differences on the different platforms. Does the experience make you want to dig deeper or click away?

Making Trade Shows Social

Social media isn't only about marketing online. Although most of this book has discussed business-to-business (B2B) marketing's new online frontier, it is also important to understand how social media can support important existing lead generation vehicles such as trade shows. Trade shows are woven into the fabric of most B2B marketing organizations and serve important lead generation and thought leadership functions. According to the Business Marketing Association, approximately 20 percent of B2B marketing spend goes to trade shows and events.[1] That's more than any other category. To get the most out of trade shows, we need to closely examine why we use them and how social media can amplify your trade show marketing goals.

Driving Trade Show Leads with Social Media

Trade shows aren't bad. The way we use them is bad.

Influence is a key difference in whether a company has to invest in trade show lead generation instead of webinar lead generation. If a company has influence over its leads and fans, then it can use that influence to drive much lower-cost webinar leads. Ideally, you would attend trade shows that provide access to an audience that your current marketing efforts have trouble influencing. Influence does not directly equate to leads, however. As anyone who has ever been to a trade show before knows, success involves far more than simply showing up. When asked what drives trade show booth traffic, many will give the lovely and ambiguous answer, "Buzz."

The truth is that trade shows have been around for a while and that many of the best ways to drive booth traffic have become commoditized over the years. Between giveaways, scavenger hunts, contests, and the like, it often seems that booth traffic is a function of execution and budget. Social media is your secret weapon to transform trade show attendees into booth visitors and leads.

Treat Trade Shows Like Comarketing

The truth is that for many B2B events, social media unlocks a secret door to extra benefits and gives exhibitors leverage that they have never enjoyed before. Regardless of the type of B2B trade show you are attending, the event organizers always want bigger and more qualified attendance. They are busy doing their own marketing to make that happen. Your goal to use trade shows and social media to catapult you further toward marketing superstardom should be to make trade shows more like comarketing. Instead of the traditional vendor-customer relationship, comarketing occurs when two complementary, and not competitive, organizations agree to work together to cross-promote each other's leads.

If you have been following the advice from previous chapters and doing the three steps at the end of each, then it is likely you have built up some decent online reach for your company. The beauty is that this online reach can be used for leverage. Before signing up for your next trade show, set a goal for discounts or upgrades. Then propose some comarketing opportunities as reasons for the discount. For example, you could agree to write a blog post about the event on your company blog or send an e-mail to your customer list about the event in exchange for a booth discount.

On top of this new leverage, many trade shows are undervaluing their online assets and tossing them in as a value-add. Use this attitude to your advantage and negotiate inbound links from the trade show websites with anchor text that connects to your unified keyword strategy. When it comes to social add-ons, negotiate with the event organizer for guest blog posts, host a Twitter chat at the event, and request a specific number of mentions on the event social network pages.

The key is to understand that as a marketer, you have more leverage than ever before when it comes to maximizing the return on investment (ROI) from trade shows. Think about the five steps of social media lead generation outlined in Chapter 2: get the basics right, maximize content discovery, create conversion ubiquity, test and fail fast, and optimize for maximum lead flow. Brainstorm trade show–related ideas that could help support any of the five steps.

Five Steps to Instantly Make Your Trade Show More Social

Trade shows are inherently social in an offline sense, but how do marketers connect these offline events with online tactics to exponentially improve results? We have five tactics that you can incorporate into your next trade show to make it instantly more social.

1. *Eliminate brochures*—The world is becoming increasingly more digital. It is time to retire the printed brochure. Yes, people do still read paper materials, but they don't like carrying them. You can still create a brochure and place a copy on a branded USB memory stick so that it is easy for people to take back to the office. Once in the office, they can simply print it out if they still want a paper version. Having a digital version creates the ability to add links to landing pages and social media profiles to support lead generation and social media reach building. But don't limit yourself to only a digital brochure. Brainstorm how you can use pages of your website, your blog, ebooks, and other resources to better influence potential customers.

2. *Make your booth content inbound*—At the core of inbound marketing is the principle that people don't want to be interrupted. Instead, they want to discover your business at the time when they are looking for the type of solution you provide. Guess what having salespeople lurking at the edge of your booth and gimmicky contests is? It isn't inbound. Instead, apply the same approach to your trade show booth that you do to your blog, ebooks, and webinars.

    Turn down the selling initially to get more traffic into the booth, but have opportunities for visitors to convert once they are in the booth. For example, have your sales team do a free assessment of the facet of their business that your product or service can solve. After that assessment, you can offer to send additional materials to improve the issues that were raised in the assessment. Collect the contact information you'll need to send along these materials. Boom! Instant trade show lead generation.

3. *Follow instead of collect*—A great salesperson will tell you that closing a deal is about establishing trust and credibility with the buyer. Take this concept and use it in your social media strategy. Retract booth

workers' hands from trying to snatch up business cards at any cost. Instead, start an in-person dialog with visitors to your booth and ask to see if their business has any social media profiles. If they do, follow or Like their profiles to get a better insight into their company and to demonstrate that you care about their business and the problems they are trying to solve. Then, go for the lead information.

4. *Personalize invites*—One of the ways that social media is powerful is that it provides insight previously not available into the needs and wants of potential customers. For example, you can use Twitter Search (Twitter.com/search) to see who is talking about an upcoming trade show and what they are hoping to get out of the event. If your booth can provide some expertise and insight into their problem, then reach out to them with a personalized invitation to visit.

5. *Crowdsource content*—People love to talk about themselves. One of the best ways to get industry influencers and current customers to spread the word is to make them actively involved in the content of your trade show booth. What if you reached out to the top 10 influencers in your industry and offered them the opportunity to give a presentation at your booth during the event? Bingo. Another comarketing opportunity. While you are trying to bring people into your booth, external speakers will help spread the word through e-mail, social media, and word of mouth to help bring their audiences into your booth. Great content and improved attendance is a win-win.

Taking Over Physical and Digital Word of Mouth

Besides leads, what is the next thing every executive wants at a trade show? The all-important buzz factor. Executives attend trade shows to close deals, but they also get to catch up on industry gossip. One thing that delights an executive almost as much as a pile of new leads is people saying, "I see you guys everywhere. People at the show can't stop talking about your new product launch."

Buzz can be a hard thing to manipulate, but as a marketer it is your job to harness as much word of mouth as possible. Online buzz translates into offline buzz and vice versa.

Example: DNS Is Sexy

Domain name systems (DNS) aren't sexy. This didn't stop the folks at Dyn, Inc. This provider of DNS and e-mail infrastructure for enterprise companies was in search of a way to leave the boring preconceptions of DNS behind. They needed to expand their reach beyond the technology geek and move upstream to those on the executive level who don't care about DNS but do care about the uptime for their online systems.

In April 2010, Dyn launched its "DNS Is Sexy" landing page,[2] which features a top 10 list of reasons DNS is sexy. It also included a video and photos of folks sporting clever T-shirts, such as "Tweet Nerdy to Me." Since then, the page has attracted more than 48,000 visitors, making it one of the most popular pages on the Dyn website.

Josh Nason, inbound marketing manager at Dyn, explains how Dyn used "DNS Is Sexy" and social media to boost trade show results: "Generally, trade shows are pretty boring. You go, you wear polo shirts, you hand out pens, etc. We broke the mold with our Dyntini events[3]— social gatherings that we sponsored at local establishments that included drinks, appetizers, and giveaway items, like the shirts. We handed out Dyntini cards that people can use for admission—handed out mainly at our booth and when we walked around and met people at these events."

Dyn used Twitter to drive awareness of the "DNS Is Sexy" campaign, as well as traffic to the company's trade show booth. Existing customers, new customers, and fans used the #DNSIsSEXY hashtag to share positive comments about Dyn and DNS. Dyn's Twitter campaign, combined with trade shows, has led to the distribution of more than 5,000 DNS Is Sexy T-shirts around the world. Dyn still receives pictures from customers and fans wearing their shirts.

After launching the "DNS Is Sexy" campaign, Dyn's distribution of Dyntini tickets increased 235 percent. Attendance was tremendous as well, with 95 percent of the tickets handed out being redeemed. More people, bigger presence, and increased sales/retention equal trade show marketing success.

The brilliant part of the "DNS Is Sexy" campaign is that it built trust with core users (technology geeks) who understood DNS, and it caused those who didn't (executives) to start asking questions.

Three Trade Show Takeaways from "DNS Is Sexy"

1. *Create a "cooler" event*—With its Dyntini events, Dyn created a trade show after-party that was way cooler than walking around a maze of booths. In the world of B2B relationship-based selling, having a place for more private decisions means a lot to your sales team.
2. *Have a big idea*—Your customers want something to believe in. "DNS Is Sexy" was the big idea that validated Dyn's end users while drawing interest from key decision makers.
3. *Use giveaways to amplify*—We are all fans. Some of us are fans of sports teams or movie stars. In the world of social media, people are fans of companies. By creating and distributing DNS Is Sexy T-shirts, Dyn was able to give their fans a way to publicly show their support for not only the big idea, but also the company itself.

Using Location to Become the Best "Party" at a Trade Show

Location-based social networks are becoming increasingly popular with consumer marketers for brick-and-mortar businesses. These networks allow users to check-in to a physical location, basically telling their online friends where they are. Location-based social networks, such as Foursquare, have been slow to be adopted by B2B marketers, and rightfully so given its focus on retail businesses. The general adoption of these networks is still only a fraction of major social media players such as LinkedIn, Twitter, and Facebook.

Location-based networks for business-to-consumer (B2C) companies really function like public online loyalty programs. Imagine if every time you scanned your supermarket loyalty card, it told all of your friends you were shopping at that store. Sure, this is extremely valuable to B2C businesses, but what about B2B? In most cases, it isn't relevant. However, there is one case where location can be a valuable tool for B2B companies: trade shows.

The goal of a trade show booth is to drive traffic and leads. One source of booth traffic is word of mouth. Think of a trade show as a college campus. Booths are like house parties on a Friday night. The trade show floor is nothing more than a collection of house parties. When you were in college, which party did you go to? The party that all of your friends were at. Location-based social networks, such as Foursquare, help prospects tell other prospects that your booth is the best "house party."

The important part of spreading the word online about the awesomeness of your trade show booth is ultimately getting booth visitors to take a second to check in. As a marketer, this is where some simple planning can pay huge dividends. Foursquare and other location-based social networks offer the ability to post specials at a location for free. Foursquare provides details on how to sign up and promote your own specials on the business section of their website: Foursquare.com/business.[4] For retail establishments, these specials are often a discount on consumer goods, such as coffee or sandwiches. So, what does a B2B company offer up at a trade show? Well, lots of things.

Your special could be an entry in a contest for an amazing prize. It could be access to a special event. Or it could even be something as simple as some free food or beverage. The offer itself doesn't matter. What matters? Rewarding booth visitors who check in. Even if you don't take the time to set up a Foursquare special, you can still simply make the offer in person as someone comes to visit your booth.

Location may not be hugely applicable for B2B companies, but when it comes to trade shows, it is another tool in your marketing superhero utility belt.

Virtual Conference

Exhibiting at trade shows is a great marketing tool. Trade shows put your business smack in the middle of a large pool of qualified prospects who can make deals in person. The problem is that in an age of budget cuts and free online information, some businesses are electing to not send employees to trade shows. The Internet provides an answer to part of the problem trade shows and marketers are facing. Although the Internet can't provide the in-person interaction of trade shows, it can provide a low-cost, community learning environment. This has been done for years by conducting webinars, which we discussed in detail in Chapter 6. In recent years, webinar platforms have evolved, and marketers have begun to host virtual conferences. These one- or two-day events function like a completely online trade show. The kicker is that, as a marketer, you can host

FIGURE 13.1 Example of a Virtual Conference

your own virtual conference for a minimal investment compared with the cost of producing a full-scale trade show.

Virtual conference software providers such as INXPO, WebEx, Citrix, and others, essentially provide software that links together webinar-like presentations with a virtual trade show floor for online networking. See Figure 13.1 for an example of what a virtual conference might look like. Virtual conferences fill an interesting gap. These online events are complementary and not competitive to trade shows. Whether you are hosting a customer conference or one based on thought leadership, your ability to use a virtual conference depends on one core element: reach. Now you understand why we wrote Chapter 5 of this book. Reach is important. The reason many businesses shell out major bucks for trade show booth space is reach. Businesses who can build reach online can leverage virtual trade shows to reduce trade show spends and build deeper connections with customers and prospects.

Michael A. Stelzner, author of the book *Launch* and founder of Social Media Examiner and Social Media Success Summit, says, "Virtual conferences are ideal for an audience that is geographically dispersed and that can't afford to travel to a physical venue. The biggest advantages of virtual conferences are the low overhead. Because you don't need to provide food, pay for convention floor space, cover travel expenses for speakers, and be constrained by 'how big the room is,' virtual conferences are an excellent alternative to physical events."

According to Stelzner, this means you can lower the ticket price for attendees and make your money on volume. Social Media Examiner holds three virtual conventions each year. Attendance ranges from 1,500 to 3,000 people at each event. These events are highly profitable for Social Media Examiner yet affordable for attendees.

Social media doesn't make trade shows obsolete. Instead it makes them more important. Trade shows provide a way to strengthen relationships with prospects that were established online. Use social media to maximize the return on your next B2B trade show by leveraging some of the strategies and examples outlined in this chapter.

Three B2B Social Media Trade Show Steps to Superstardom

1. *Take online reach offline*—Social media reach isn't limited to generating only online leads. Instead leverage your social media assets such as your blog, Facebook Page, LinkedIn Group, and more, to drive traffic to your trade show booth to increase offline leads and engagement. Starting 90 days before your next trade show, launch a contest on your social media channels to give away a pass to the event. Use this contest to identify social media connections that are actively interested and may be attending the event. Determine a method of ongoing communication with these prospects using e-mail, a LinkedIn Group, and more. Test different offers and messages to maximize the number of people from this group who visit your trade show booth.

2. *Become a comarketing partner*—Don't let trade show event organizers get away with highway robbery. Instead show them that your company is a valuable partner in helping them promote their event. Establish a comarketing relationship in which you offer some promotion to your audience in exchange for a booth discount and a free ticket to be used in the contest mentioned in step 1. Be sure to report on the cost savings that were generated due to your social media reach.

3. *Socialize your trade show*—Follow the five methods outlined in this chapter for socializing your trade show. For each of the five methods, have in place some method for storing these points of engagement in the lead record for each booth visit, even if this means entering them manually. Measure how these tactics affected booth attendance compared with attendance of previous years. In addition, note the lead-to-customer rate for these trade show leads to determine whether this extra engagement increased the revenue generated from the event.

Run a B2B Social Media Marketing Team Like a Start-Up

We have looked at many of the ways that social media can drive leads, which can ultimately increase sales at business-to-business (B2B) companies. Now we want to put forth a model for building a different kind of marketing team to optimize the lead generation process. What if the social media team within your marketing department acts like a start-up company. Start-ups are passionate, are nimble, and get things done. They are used to operating on tight budgets, but they know when it is time to ask for funding. Start-ups operate on shorter goal cycles and have flat organizational charts to make it easier for collaboration. Oh, and there is usually a dog under someone's desk.

Although this small-team approach is not a new idea for marketing departments, it is pretty rare within a sales-driven, or even product-driven, B2B company.

It All Starts with Passion

A marketing superstar brings passion to the job every day. Social media without passion is push marketing. When an entrepreneur starts a new company, he or she does so with a great deal of passion. He or she is usually looking at long nights, time away from family, and strained finances. One motivator through the early days of the start-up is their passion for the idea. The entrepreneur knows that others will follow along once they glimpse the grand idea.

Displaying your passion for your company's product is what sets you apart.

Corporate marketers generally are not known for their passion for their company or its products or services. Large corporations are more known for their bureaucracy, office politics, and clock-watchers. This complacency reinforces the status quo. In our uncertain times, you should strive for disruption. This is the path to standing out and achieving success.

A company opening itself to the world via social media requires a great amount of transparency. A marketer who is a clock-watcher will not have the same impact in this environment as one who is passionate. One of the easiest ways to get frustrated with a corporate bureaucracy is to try to start a social media program.

You must make a commitment to be passionate about social media every single day. Everyone goes through cycles of not having the best attitude toward his or her job, but all members on a social media team needs to do their best to remain on the positive side of the cycle as much as possible. Whether using words, audio, or video, passion—or more specifically, a lack of passion—comes through.

Start every day with the following mantra:

I love my job.
I am awesome.
My team is awesome.
Our products make a difference.
What can I do to make a difference today?
I am a marketing superstar.
Watch me soar!

If that is too self-agey for you, what about starting each day with a positive attitude and doing your best to stay positive all day long. Don't waste your time, energy, and focus on being negative. Look for the positive outcomes.

Buyers at companies want to do business with others who believe in their products and services. Passion is one big step above just believing in a product. This is in an age when many people already distrust marketing. A passionate approach through social media can make a huge difference in convincing prospects of the viability of a company's products as a business solution.

"An insatiable, unquenchable desire to study, read, grow, risk, integrate, experiment, and *learn*," is how Rick Short, director of marketing communications at Indium Corporation describe a marketing superstar. "Without this, a marketer will be average. I am not paid to be average. I only win when I and my team are above average. Therefore, I *must* know more, be more capable, be faster, and be more powerful than my competition."

Where Does Passion Come From?

It doesn't come from the top of a mountain or the inside of a fruit. Passion comes from a strong belief that your company's products are the answer— and not just an answer, but *the* answer. It also comes from being fully committed to your company. This type of attitude can be a benefit in a lot of areas of your work life.

It is easy to develop passion around a start-up because of the small team and the working environment. It can be challenging to translate that experience to a social media team working within a corporate marketing department. Start by removing barriers to getting things done. Rather than banish the team to individual offices with walls, doors, and dedicated spaces, create a social media command center. Although it would be great to create a true command center with large monitors to watch the social media world flow by in real time the way Dell does it,[1] it is also beneficial to merely be in the same room.

Sharing an office space allows sharing of ideas and the spreading of passion. Your team can work together to manage social media profiles, develop creative ideas, and feed off each other's passion for the product. It also makes it easier to talk to other people in the company, together. Rather than go to a product manager's office, bring that person into the social media lair and conduct an interview as a group. This can create content that might not have existed if only one person did it. A successful group project like this helps build passion as well, because everyone understands that it is better than if any individual member had conducted the interview himself or herself.

A passionate team approaches the world as a cohesive unit.

This is definitely required for social media. Whether team members came from marketing, public relations, or customer service, every-one is responsible for promoting and protecting the company and its brand. The passion for that job shows through in every aspect of their work.

Knowing When to Ship

Best-selling author Seth Godin describes shipping as getting it out the door, making a difference at work, or contributing your art and vision and expertise and passion to a project.[2] Understanding what shipping means is part of becoming a marketing superstar. Although this metaphor comes from the product side of the business, the idea of knowing when to ship has become an important part of the agile methodology.

It is partly about literally shipping projects, but it is more about using your passion and confidence in your ideas to overcome resistance. We are all distracted by meetings, phone calls, and daily responsibilities that prevent us from being awesome. According to Godin, a part of our brain called the amygdala, or our primitive lizard brain, also prevents us from being remarkable because evolution does not want us to stand out. So not only is your office environment keeping you from shipping great ideas, but your brain is conspiring against you too.

Start-ups overcome these issues by maintaining small teams, limiting meetings, and setting short deadlines. Without the pressure of huge product releases, major project presentations, and the internal desire to maintain the status quo, start-ups have the freedom to be creative and push the limits of what is possible.

Shipping a project doesn't mean putting out an unacceptable project. Instead it means shipping a minimally viable project and then improving on it through iteration.

B2B marketers need to learn what it means to "ship it." On a very tactical level, it means not getting caught up in reviews, approvals, and other corporate trappings of inaction and moving forward with social media projects to drive revenue. On a much higher level, it is about being remarkable as a marketer. The path to marketing superstar is learning to ship and teaching others the value of it.

Don't be afraid to share a big idea. Mediocre ideas do not resonate with prospects. Mediocre ideas do not break through the clutter. Mediocre ideas are not game changers.

It Becomes Agile Marketing Anyway

Corporate marketing is not known for its ability to move quickly or to review the latest reports to make short-term course corrections. Alan Belniak was a product manager in an agile development environment for PTC. He transferred into the marketing department, where he is the director of social media marketing. He explains how most corporate marketing works, which is totally contrary to the way products are managed at the same company.

"When we do budget planning at the beginning of our fiscal year and we are trying to forecast how we are going to spend our last $1,000 eleven and a half months from now, I raise my hand and say, is it really pragmatic to think that we know how we are going to spend our last $1,000, when the reality is that I don't really know what I am doing three months from now. We are going to meet six months through the year to do a course correction and rehash, which means that we are doing agile marketing anyway."[3]

Three Principles of Agile Marketing

1. *Sprints*—The agile framework is often based on a monthly schedule. In programming, these are called sprints, but when the entire year is based on monthly sprints—that is, if that's the normal speed—there is really no need to call them that. Social media data are usually reported on a monthly basis. In some instances with larger brands or industries, monthly measurements seem too far apart, and weekly reporting is more appropriate. Keep in mind that this is in an organization where a community manager is monitoring in real time, so the reporting is for others, not the listening and engaging team.

2. *Short meetings*—Another aspect of an agile environment is the short meeting, sometimes called a scrum. The idea is that nobody wants to waste a lot of time in long corporate meetings reading from PowerPoint slides. How many of your days slip completely away because you spend them entirely in meetings, getting nothing decided and preventing you from getting your work done. Agile-style meetings are less than 10 minutes and can be scheduled at a

time when people don't have a lot of time. These meetings are to make sure everyone is on the same page.

If the social media team is in the same room, these meetings are even easier. Once a day, take 10 minutes, turn the chairs toward one another and chat about what's going on. This is not a status. It is not a let's look good in front of management meeting. It is about keeping the team informed of anything that they need to do their jobs better today.

The emphasis is on today, or even right now.

Something might be happening on Facebook, and it is relevant to update the blog. These meetings are meant to be efficient and about helping get things done.

3. *Review for optimization*—You should look through your monthly reports as soon as possible after the end of the month to identify whether any course corrections are needed. Although the team can make minor corrections during the course of the month, make sure you are tracking the right metrics to measure your goals. Since we have focused on generating leads for your B2B company, we will review this section in that context.

Examine every update on a social media profile for the number of clicks it drove to your landing page. Look at what kind of content drove the most traffic. How does that traffic relate to leads generated? Break this down by platform, time of day, type of content, landing page details, and how many fields to fill out. Once there is a baseline for all these variables, they can be compared from month to month. The types of updates that drive the most leads are the ones that should be increased the following month. And it can also tell you what to stop doing.

When It's Time to Look for Funding

B2B companies are spending a greater percentage of their marketing budget on online marketing, including social media. Online activities accounted for 7 percent of the B2B marketing mix in 2008. This is set to reach 12 percent by 2013.[4] Everything is going digital, and social media is a big component of that. Marketers start to wonder how to get their share of that increased budget. Within many organizations, social media might be a line item in a marketing budget, and there's just not enough awareness to justify the increased spending.

By taking a page from the start-up launch playbook, the social media team led by a marketing superstar needs to market itself and its ability to drive business outcomes so that it can have more visibility come budget time. Once companies start generating leads using social media, it becomes easier to request a greater part of the marketing budget. With social media success comes your success, and that makes it easier to ask for a larger budget.

The sales department turns those leads into sales, right? So the sales force can become an ally when that happens. If the company has a customer relationship management (CRM) solution for tracking leads, make sure the social media leads are properly categorized so that they can be reported on. Salespeople are known to chat with others, so be sure to remind them about the number of leads that have closed into customers from social media.

What's the Exit Strategy?

Start-ups are all about the exit strategy. The choices are to sell out after a successful product launch or to look for additional investors so that the company can hang on until it is time for an initial public offering (IPO). A social media marketing team can also leverage its success at helping grow the business and develop its own exit strategy.

Once a social media team has successfully generated leads for the B2B company, what's next? There are several directions this exit strategy can take, and they should all be considered in building a team. Good managers like to hire good people and look out for their careers. Exceptional team members need to be rewarded, but traditional corporate promotions may not be of interest to them. Someone who enjoys engaging with customers through social media may not want a higher-level position where more of their time is spent managing people and processes.

As a marketer growing an internal social media team; it is important to select the right people. Whether they are from marketing, corporate communications, or customer service, each team member needs to fit the position they currently hold and be a fit for the next position up the ladder. This is critical as the team scales to handle more social media engagement and content development.

One way to approach the growth of the team is to consider naming team leaders and breaking the team into smaller teams. This gives the exceptional members the ability to have more responsibility, yet still maintain their preferred daily tasks. In a corporate structure, these team leaders can be recognized with promotions. As others in the organization interact with the new social media teams, they begin to view the teams as separate groups, almost like their own spin-off start-up.

Another way to approach these spin-off teams is to have them focus on the next thing on the horizon. What if the new team focused on mobile social strategy or how to stand out as a company on Google+? This group becomes the social media scouts and watches for what is next. It doesn't take away from their traditional social media role because they have been selected to watch the future and analyze it for the marketing organization.

An agile social media team is an ideal model for a function that is changing so fast. A small, passionate team sitting in one room, with daily short meetings to meet monthly goals, can set the standard for marketing in your company. Stock the fridge with Mountain Dew and get the team to work.

Three B2B Social Media Start-Up Steps to Superstardom

1. *Embrace your passion*—One of the best ways to increase your passion for your company is to fully understand your products or services. Schedule time once every two weeks with a product engineer, product manager, or technical support personnel to learn the products inside and out. Every 90 days, schedule time to have hands-on use of the product with a customer. Seeing the solutions provided by your product directly from your customers will amplify and focus your passion.
2. *Get agile. Now!*—Set a date for your team to begin working using agile methods. In the two weeks before the transition, hold a couple of training meetings so that everyone understands the process once your first sprint starts.
3. *Learn to ship and iterate*—Being agile is about consistently releasing new work and improving it over time. Set aggressive deadlines to force you and your team to ship earlier than you have on similar projects in the past. These shorter timelines increase the velocity of your projects.

10 B2B Social Media Roadblocks

Congratulations on making it to Chapter 15. If you have made it this far, and you have completed the activities along the way, you are on your way to becoming a marketing superstar by using social media to generate leads. This book has been positive and straightforward about the things that you need to do to succeed, but we understand that social media does not exist in a vacuum. In every business-to-business (B2B) organization, there are roadblocks that must be overcome. Each one of these comes with suggestions about how to clear these roadblocks from your path. You may not encounter all of these, but you likely have already experienced some.

1. Legal Wants Full Approval—Of *Everything*

Marketers don't usually have much contact with the legal department. Attorneys look to mitigate risk in all situations involving your company. Although they may need to be in the loop to approve traditional advertising, this is a process that can be managed. Often, they are looking for product claims that cannot be substantiated.

The frequency of producing new ads, whether for print or digital, does not compare to the content-creating machine of a marketing department using social media to drive leads. *There is no reasonable way for the legal department to approve every blog post, tweet, Facebook update, LinkedIn Answer, forum post, and comment response.* Once they get wind of a social media program, their first response will be to say that they need full approval of everything.

Clear This Roadblock Get legal involved as soon as possible when developing a social media plan. Create an approval playbook in conjunction with legal where everyone agrees on the "no approval" updates. Train all social media team members on legal concerns and issues of risk so that everyone is on the same page as far as legal issues are concerned.

2. Social Network Access Is Blocked

According to a 2011 survey of chief information officers (CIOs), 31 percent of companies with more than 100 employees block employee access from social networking sites.[1] Rather than view these sites as extensions of employees' business networks that can provide information and resources to make employees more efficient, sites such as Facebook and YouTube are seen as time wasters. These directives are driven by maintaining employee efficiency or a need to limit network resources. But B2B company executives need to acknowledge the value and importance of these connections to extend the company reach and to share remarkable content. These are two ideas that generate leads using social media.

In addition, many companies have adopted social media messaging in a traditional, outbound style, and their employees are unable to communicate with customers if they do not have access to social sites.

Clear This Roadblock If access is blocked at your B2B company, determine who is behind the decision and what their concerns are. Address these concerns with examples and benefits. Time wasting and inefficiency are not valid concerns for most employees. An employee who would spend his time on Facebook rather than do his work is probably surfing the Web instead of doing his work now. This is a people problem, not a FarmVille problem. And the company can't block the entire Internet.

Cross-posting information on employee's personal social media channels, including blogs, can increase the chance of finding prospects. E-mails and mobile-optimized content can also break through this barrier.

3. Executive Support Is Lacking

By now, all B2B executives have heard stories of the benefits of social media. They just may not understand how it helps their company and how it affects the bottom line. Customers, competitors, trade media, and industry organizations are all tweeting, updating, and blogging, many without an obvious financial return to show for it.

C-suite executives are known for their conservative approach to business, and are unwilling to try something new until it is no longer new. When those executives run B2B companies, that only accentuates that conservatism. A good bit of that attitude comes from the company's customers, as the success of their company may be riding on the purchase of new computer software or warehouse logistics system.

Clear This Roadblock Remember Chapter 4 and the calculation of return on investment (ROI)? That shows business value in terms that executives understand: dollars. Create a pilot project where all costs of customer acquisition are accurately accounted for and all revenue is based on the total lifetime value of a customer. The leads that you generate with these metrics in place will demonstrate the value of social media to your business.

4. The Customer Base Is Not Attuned to Social Media

There are companies and industries where social media has not yet gained traction, and no matter how many statistics cite otherwise, our experience finds that there are still many B2B companies that have not added any social media to their marketing mix. Certain regulated industries have been reluctant to fully embrace social media as a way to connect with partners and customers. Maybe the purchasing decision is based on a long list of factors that cannot be influenced.

Clear This Roadblock Influence the influencers. Find the adjacencies. Gather customer testimonials and post them on the company blog. Use social tools to create custom information that is sent directly to prospects; this information could be a video of a product manager providing solutions for the customer, for example. Use the ideas and tools of social media, even if you don't use the networks.

5. But I Have a Real Job to Do

Nobody said marketing superstardom was going to be easy. Do you think Brad Pitt just gets out of bed every morning, tousles his hair, and is on his way? Oh wait, he probably does. So not only do you need to spend a little more time on your hair each morning, but you have all those meetings to attend, plans to write, reports to review, and so on. How are you ever going to start creating content to drive leads? You are not a blogger. You have a real job to do.

Clear This Roadblock   Organization, time management, and planning will help you with this one. You didn't get this far by not having those skills already. Start by creating a blog idea file. Every time something occurs to you that would help a customer or prospect, put it in the file. Create a custom search column in HootSuite or TweetDeck and spend about 15 minutes in the middle of the day scrolling through it. Mark tweets as favorites or bookmark posts for later review. This will keep you up on your industry and give you more blog post ideas. Once a week or every two weeks combine the two of these things and create an editorial calendar. This will make it easier to publish relevant content on a consistent basis.

6. It Is Free, Right?

Many social media platforms are available to use free of charge, but that doesn't mean they are free. As we just reviewed, it takes time, and sometimes lots of it, to create the content to share on these platforms. Many platforms also have paid features, as well as paid advertising models that help increase the reach of a company's content.

Managers can accept moving forward with social media when they think their department will not incur any additional cost. Driving additional sales without any additional expense is the perfect model for our time, but unfortunately, this is not the case. Everyone wants to do more for less, and free is even better. There are budget implications with all approaches provided in this book. When someone spends time creating content to share on social networks, there is something else that they are not doing.

Clear This Roadblock   Everyone knows that there is cost to employees doing work. Many managers ignore an in-house cost versus an out-of-pocket expense in their budget. They think that they are paying employees to be there anyway, so there is no incremental cost to charging that employee with additional tasks. A definitive budget is required to calculate ROI, and that will need to include the cost of employees. By accurately figuring out the costs required for customer acquisition using social media, not only will it make the case that none of this is free, but it will also bust the myth of free.

7. We Need the Right People for the Task

Social media success requires a variety of people, each with specialized skills. Teams usually start small and can even be a team of one. Creative marketers look for skills within existing employees so that they can leverage their abilities and borrow some of their time instead of hiring new employees.

If all the skills required for a full-blown social media team were provided by a single person each, the team would include a strategist, Web developer, writer, photographer, videographer, community manager, search engine optimization (SEO) expert, analyst, educator, public speaker, and politician.

It is unlikely that you will get approval to launch with a team of this size. And many of these skills are complementary, so people will be able to do multiple tasks. If it is only you, dear marketer, you will have to play to your strengths and learn as you go. With power comes great responsibility.

Clear This Roadblock   Before hiring anyone to join the social media team, or enlisting the help from others in your department or other departments, develop a clear strategy based on determining where your customers are engaging online. A core part of any social media plan is a regularly updated blog that can tell the story of the company, its products, and its solutions using words, pictures, video, audio, and graphics. These skills exist in many people, but you may find that product or company knowledge is more important. The right people think a certain way and understand the value of publishing content and engaging online.

8. We Have Always Done It *This* Way

Unless you work for a start-up that moves fast, every B2B marketing department has people who don't like change. You can probably identify them by the newspaper comics hanging on the wall above their desks. They are reluctant to try anything new because what has always been done has worked. Your company has always brought in new customers using trade advertising, attending trade shows, and sending direct mail. Although nobody is advocating these tactics be dropped without analysis, you will find that your ability to analyze the success of many traditional marketing tactics is lacking.

And just because you have not gone out of business by doing things the way you have always done them is no reason to take that chance. Take a look at the music, publishing, and movie businesses who ignored change for so long and are now thrashing about to figure out how to survive in a new age.

Clear This Roadblock   In this buyer-centric world, a change in marketing is required or there will be no new stream of customers. You must find ways to build relationships with offers that are valuable to prospects. Show your grumpy colleague the power of social media using a search engine to look for relevant keywords for your business. Point out how many results are blogs rather than corporate websites. Search for the same terms on Twitter and add the words "looking for" or "recommendations" to find prospects on the social network.

9. The Network Admin Is a Debbie Downer

Many social media programs started with marketers or communications pros. This second Internet revolution completely bypassed the network administrator and the information technology (IT) department. When you needed your first company website—if you are that old—the IT department was required. The site needed to be written by a programmer and it needed to be hosted somewhere. There was no way around these technical requirements, even if you hired an outside firm. And that is still the case. Everything on the social web exists as a hosted solution that does not require internal technical support.

Network admins control everything about a network: what you do, how you do it, and what device you use—but not with social media. They were hired because they are control freaks, and they have trouble letting go. Cloud-based computing is becoming more accepted among corporate IT staff because they still control it. Social media is too much out of their control. They want to build in-house solutions. Why would they install an open-source blog platform such as WordPress when they can build their own propriety blogging software?

Clear This Roadblock   Marketers have tended to install various social media programs, review paid solutions from nonapproved vendors, and move forward without the blessing of the network admin. From a marketing solutions perspective, there is no reason to get the approval of IT to launch a social media campaign. In an environment where control of the network can be an issue, you should make friends with the IT folks. Any good social media practitioner needs to know some HTML and other basic technical skills as they build those relationships with IT. Learn a little bit and go ask someone in IT a question. This is like trying to speak French when in France. You get points for trying.

10. You Don't Know Where to Start

Everything you have read makes so much sense, but your head is spinning. It's like you just went to an awesome conference, took pages and pages of notes, and now have to make sense of it all and find a place to start. Do you pick a platform, create a profile, and start? Do you write a strategy? Do you talk to customers? What about your boss? Do you talk to him or her and get approval to start?

Clear This Roadblock   We have been focusing on lead generation, and that is where this starts. What remarkable offers will you present to your prospects so that they will take the action you want and become leads. If these calls to action will live in the footer of each and every blog post, get busy planning the blog. This means design, hosting, content strategy, editorial calendar, and identification of other company bloggers.

LESSONS FROM A MARKETING SUPERSTAR

Name: Beth Comstock
Title: Chief Marketing Officer
Company: General Electric
Years in Position: 3.5

What is the greatest social media/marketing success at your company? Our highest-profile social media success was the GE Ecomagination Challenge, which represents a $200 million innovation experiment where businesses, entrepreneurs, innovators, and students shared their best ideas on how to build next-generation (1) smart grid and (2) home energy solutions.

More than 70,000+ community members discussed and voted on 1,000+ ideas for home energy management and 3,000+ ideas for smart grid. Ideas came from kids as young as 10 and entrepreneurs as old as 90. Ideas came in from about 150 countries.

We ended up funding a wide spectrum of ideas that create and use energy resources sustainably.

As for harder metrics, we'll be able to quantify our social efforts because we made actual investments in a number of companies. That said, the investments are less than a year old, so we're still a couple of years from seeing the returns.

What is the biggest roadblock in executing social media strategy? I think we're finding that scalability is the chief roadblock in executing on a global social media strategy. We're in the process of baking social into the daily operating rhythm of 300,000+ employees globally; that's not easy, especially when you consider the complexity of the radically different business lines that we have operating in radically different cultures. One day we're thinking about how social impacts the aviation business in the U.S. and the next day we're thinking about how to engage Brazilian consumers around smart grid.

We're embarking on a series of long-term conversations, and we're excited by the ways that both our businesses and online communities can benefit from this increasingly open dialog.

What is the single most important trait of a B2B marketer? At the end of the day, you're in business to delight your customers. It really doesn't matter whether you're in the B2B or B2C space—get as close to your end users as you can and listen to their needs.

You'll realize more quickly what doesn't work and apply those insights to create products, services, and experiences that *do* delight.

Three Clearing Roadblock Steps to Superstardom

1. *Determine your roadblocks*—B2B marketers are used to encountering roadblocks along the way to success. Because it is new and different, social media causes even more roadblocks than traditional marketing. Determine your three most difficult roadblocks and make a list of five steps each that are required to overcome them. Establish a timeline over the next 90 days to accomplish each step required to overcome each roadblock.

2. *Predict your roadblocks*—Roadblocks will not just occur at the beginning of a social media program. There will be additional roadblocks that occur once social media is implemented. Based on your company culture, anticipate three potential roadblocks that you expect to encounter once your social media program has begun. You must stop these from happening before they occur. List three steps that you will need to prevent these roadblocks from happening.

3. *Convince your colleagues*—Sometimes roadblocks are people. Your boss is probably not one, because that was your first step in the approval process. But you could encounter trouble if others in your organization don't support the social media plan. Name three colleagues who do not understand how to use social media for lead generation and create a short slide deck (five slides or fewer) to show them how it works.

The Best Time Ever!

Now is the time.
It is the time when the rubber meets the road.
It is the time when learning is replaced by doing.
Now is the best time ever to be a marketer.

Ignore the economy, the critics, and the doubting executives. Today, more than any other time, you have the tools and knowledge to enable your business to win. Arts and crafts time is over. You are leading a revolution. A revolution in which creativity and analytical thinking collide. A revolution that transforms your business. A revolution that shows your company and the world the marketing superstar you really are.

We have taught you how to rise above the hugs and kisses too often associated with social media marketing. We have empowered you with a treasure trove of tactics, ideas, and best practices.

Our job is over. Your job is just starting.

It isn't going to be easy. Being great never is. However, it won't be any more difficult than being mediocre.

You are better than mediocre.

Looking back at our discussion of social media return on investment (ROI) in Chapter 4, it is clear that many marketers will be asking for some of this financial data for the first time, and there may be some resistance to these requests. However, once your resisting boss understands that you need this information and data to become a better steward of the marketing budget and to drive more revenue for the business, resistance transforms into respect. Without the support of your company's leadership, great marketing is nearly impossible. You are too brilliant to simply be a tactical executor of a mediocre strategy.

History and innovation are on a collision course right in front of you. Your skills combined with social media tools create an opportunity never before seen in marketing. Don't waste it.

Social Media *Marketing* Is about Lead Generation

Social media enables online conversations. As a B2B *marketer,* never lose sight that social media's primary role is to generate leads. Customer service, public relations, and community building are all important functions of social media, but they aren't marketing functions. Your job as a marketer is to drive new leads for your business and better engage existing leads.

Keep this book at hand as a reference. We wrote it to be one. Although lead generation, search, and measuring return on investment (ROI) are the foundation to your business-to-business (B2B) social media success, the tactical chapters, including those on offers, blogging, Twitter, Facebook, and LinkedIn, will provide substance for a successful social media strategy.

Always remember that great solution-based content fuels each step of the social media lead generation process. From ebooks to tweets and everything in between, content matters.

Be a Storyteller Who Uses Data

No longer do you need to hold up your finger to see which way the wind is blowing. Social media has helped usher in an age of marketing in which data are abundant. Visits, conversion rates, referral traffic, and the host of other data points available serve as powerful levers.

These data aren't only about stacked bar graphs and end-of-the-quarter reports, though. These data are the kernels of knowledge that grow into a remarkable story. To use data to influence your marketing content, conduct analysis to answer these important questions:

- How do visitors read and interact with my content?
- What offers convert prospects into customers at the highest rate?
- What are the most popular keywords my target audience is searching for?
- What data do I have about my target audience that would help them solve their problems?

Use data for storytelling. Data bolster credibility and validate assumptions.

Second Is the First Loser

The strategic and tactical guidance outlined in this book will be a major boost in your trajectory toward marketing superstardom. However, that trajectory will be diminished greatly if not used in conjunction with some key principles of the social web. From talking about running a marketing team like a start-up to outlining successful social media marketing tactics, agility has been a clear and common theme of tactics outlined in this book. Agility is a core principle for marketing success on the Web. It is important to understand that the Web has caused a fundamental shift in market share distribution.

Before the Web, a given industry would have one leader in market share, followed by a handful of companies that also had large shares of the market and that would battle one another on a path to first place. That is, a handful of companies controlled the majority of market share for an industry. In the age of the Internet, markets have become winner take all. Look at many Web industries: Amazon holds a massive lead in online shopping, and Google holds a similar lead in search engine market share. B2B online marketing works the same way.

Second place is the first loser. The company that moves first to leverage the Web for B2B marketing will have a clear and distinct advantage over the competition. Let's say that you start a business blog for your company today and blog once a week. That is 52 blog posts a year. If your competitors waited a year to start their blog, they would be 52 posts behind you before they even started. As we learned in the business blogging chapter, blogging is one of the best ways to increase the number of pages on your website, which generates more leads.

The Internet rewards first movers. First movers generate more traffic. They accrue more social media connections. They build more inbound links. It doesn't matter if you are getting started with your B2B social media strategy or expanding an existing one; the key is to remember that it is more important to launch something sooner, and then iterate and improve on it over time. Perfection is a foolish and losing pursuit.

Striving for absolute perfection will get you nothing better than second place.

Useless Metrics

Never lose sight of why you are executing a marketing strategy: to drive leads and revenue for the business.

You have made it to the very end of this book. We spent an entire chapter addressing B2B social media roadblocks. Yes, those will be common challenges in your fight to become a superstar marketer, but they actually won't be the biggest impediment in your path.

WARNING   Don't get caught up in meaningless metrics! Followers, fans, open rates, and impressions are useless.

Too many marketers print flashy graphs of impressions, mentions, and heaps of other "marketing junk" to show off their social media marketing expertise. These metrics don't matter. They won't gain the respect of the leaders of your company.

Instead, they merely reinforce the idea that marketing is about arts and crafts and that marketers should be left to manage trade show arrangements while the "real" departments work on growing the business. The mere idea of this should send your blood to a near-boiling point.

From strategy to tactics to the marketing tools you implement, ensure that you are reporting and optimizing for one thing: revenue. Revenue for B2B companies can be a lagging indicator due to long sales cycles. This is why it is important to use leads as a predictive indicator of revenue. A key way to report on this is to have a clear understanding of your lead-to-customer rate. If you know that, on average, you generate 1 customer for every 200 leads and you know that the average revenue of a customer is $7,000, it becomes pretty easy to project revenue from specific marketing channels. For example, if social media generated 1,400 leads in a quarter, then it would be fair to project an estimated revenue of $49,000 from the social media marketing efforts of that quarter given our previous lead-to-customer rate.

Marketing superstars speak in one language and one language only: dollars.

Build a reporting infrastructure to easily know the expense and results of your social media marketing efforts in dollars. This simple step will ensure that you kick all of the meaningless metrics to the curb.

The Beginning, Not the End

As this book ends, your marketing journey is only beginning. Social media isn't a silver bullet. It is one aspect of marketing that must be integrated with other channels for the best results. Examine your current marketing strategy. Determine how to integrate social media with existing lead generation programs to lower costs per lead and improve marketing ROI.

Don't stop now.

Success doesn't occur in the time it takes to read this book.

You are a superstar. Now is *your* time to make everyone in your company believe it.

Acknowledgments

Writing a book is tough. It is easy to say that you're going to write a book, but a different story to actually pour 60,000 words out of your mind. We did it. However, this book would *never* have happened without the support, guidance, and inspiration of others.

First and foremost, we would like to thank our families, who tolerated the lonely and grinding process of writing a book. Without them it would never have gotten past being an idea.

Kipp would personally like to thank: His wife, Tera, for her unwavering support, love, and keen editing eye; the Hickle and Bodnar families, for their love and encouragement; Corey Strimer, for his friendship and consistently wise advice; and all of the brilliant marketers he works with at HubSpot, especially Mike Volpe and Jeanne Hopkins, for being great marketers and remarkable leaders. In addition, a huge thank you goes to Dan Zarrella, who encouraged this project from the beginning. Thanks and gratitude go to the original inbound marketers and HubSpot cofounders Brian Halligan and Dharmesh Shah for assembling the best team of marketers in the world.

Jeff would personally like to thank: Stephanie Styons, for supporting my social media ideas; David B. Thomas, for his support and friendship; Malia Ott, for providing me opportunity and connections; Kathy Bushman, for listening to me on long plane rides; SocialMediaB2B.com contributing writers Adam Holden-Bache and Karlie Justus, who always seemed to write a blog post when I needed it most; all of our guest writers, including Amanda O'Brien and Umberto Milletti; everyone who ever read a post, commented, retweeted, liked, posted to LinkedIn, shared via e-mail, or plussed what we wrote. And to everyone who ever made me feel like an Internet celebrity by telling me how much they liked our site and appreciated all of our content.

Over the course of our adventure in business-to-business (B2B) social media we have learned from and been inspired by a countless number of bright minds. We take a second to thank some of them: Ann Handley, Jason Falls, Wayne Sutton, Jim Tobin, Ryan Boyles, Tim Washer, Kyle Flaherty, and the dynamo that is Shannon Vargo and her team at John Wiley & Sons, Inc.

A huge thanks to Allison Satterfield of Studio You for her amazing photography skills.

Last, but not least, we thank you, the B2B marketer. You are changing the future of marketing and business! This book exists only because of your inspiration and brilliance.

About the Authors

Kipp Bodnar, Inbound Marketing Strategist, HubSpot

Kipp Bodnar is Inbound Marketing Strategist at HubSpot, the inbound marketing software leader that provides integrated tools for marketers to generate and manage leads online. Kipp leads a team of marketers who guide and execute HubSpot's inbound marketing content strategy. This includes creating content for Blog.HubSpot.com, webinars, ebooks, social media, and other channels to help educate marketers and generate leads.

Kipp is an experienced social media marketer who cofounded SocialMediaB2B.com, the leading online resource for social media's impact on B2B marketing. He also writes on his personal blog DigitalCapitalism .com, as well as guest postings on other leading marketing blogs.

He lives in Boston with his loving wife, two hyperactive beagles, and good rye whiskey that serves as antifreeze for the long New England winters.

Jeffrey L. Cohen, Social Strategies, Radian6

Jeffrey L. Cohen is a Social Strategist at Radian6, a Salesforce.com company. Radian6's social media monitoring software helps businesses listen, discover, measure, and engage in conversations across the social web. Jeff works with enterprise companies to help assess their social media strategy and adoption, and advises them on how social media marketing, communications, and engagement can help them meet their business objectives.

With more than 20 years' experience, Jeff has provided strategic market-ing counsel to B2B and B2C companies on both the client and agency sides. Jeff is also Managing Editor and cofounder of SocialMediaB2B.com, the lead-ing online resource for social media's impact on B2B marketing.

He lives in Durham, North Carolina, with his two kids and overlooking a wooded backyard.

Notes

Chapter 1

1. www.thestrategyweb.com/study-ceos-say-that-marketers-lack-business-credibility

Chapter 3

1. https://adwords.google.com/select/KeywordToolExternal

Chapter 4

1. www.convinceandconvert.com/social-media-roi/the-5-reasons-most-companies-arent-measuring-social-media

Chapter 5

1. www.hubspot.com/state-of-inbound-marketing

Chapter 6

1. www.youtube.com/watch?v=exmwSxv7XJI
2. www.google.com/support/webmasters/bin/answer.py?answer=80472

Chapter 7

1. http://radio-weblogs.com/0001011/2004/10/19.html#a8431
2. http://socialmediab2b.com/2011/01/top-10-b2b-comedy-videos
3. http://blogs.forbes.com/ericsavitz/2011/07/08/apple-canaccord-ups-target-sees-strong-ipod-iphone-sales
4. http://blog.bitly.com/post/9887686919/you-just-shared-a-link-how-long-will-people-pay

Chapter 8

1. www.leadformix.com/blog/2010/06/facebook-and-twitter-not-for-generating-b2b-leads
2. http://blog.hubspot.com/blog/tabid/6307/bid/10437/Study-LinkedIn-Is-More-Effective-for-B2B-Companies.aspx
3. http://growyourbiz.kodak.com/growyourbiz/post/?ID=5601005365834642758

Chapter 9

1. http://techcrunch.com/2011/07/18/dont-drink-and-power-use
2. http://socialmediab2b.com/2009/10/laura-fitton-pistachio-twitter-b2b
3. http://blog.sysomos.com/2011/06/02/how-people-currently-share-pictures-on-twitter
4. http://socialmediab2b.com/2011/07/b2b-twitter-hashtag-stuffing-data
5. www.edisonresearch.com/home/archives/2011/05/the_social_habit_2011.php
6. http://socialmediab2b.com/2011/03/talking-twitter-with-ann-handley-marketingprofs
7. http://twitter.com/#!/FlukeCorp/status/88623784944340992
8. http://twitter.com/#!/digikey/status/99192947664359424
9. www.sysomos.com/insidetwitter/engagement
10. http://blog.sysomos.com/2011/06/02/how-people-currently-share-pictures-on-twitter
11. www.flickr.com/photos/theboeingcompany/5958968026

Chapter 10

1. http://socialmediab2b.com/2010/05/cisco-facebook-page
2. www.socialbakers.com/blog/147-how-often-should-you-post-on-your-facebook-pages
3. www.facebook.com/CienaCorp?sk=app_101393123286933
4. www.facebook.com/mailchimp?sk=app_100265896690345
5. www.comscore.com/Press_Events/Press_Releases/2011/5/U.S._Online_Display_Advertising_Market_Delivers_1.1_Trillion_Impressions_in_Q1_2011
6 http://ads.ak.facebook.com/ads/FacebookAds/Sponsored_Stories_Guide_042511.pdf
7. www.tbgdigital.com/archive/exclusive-target-facebook-fans-for-44-cheaper-registrations-says-tbg-digital-test
8. www.facebook.com/networksolutions?sk=app_142371818162

Chapter 11

1. www.radicati.com/wp/wp-content/uploads/2010/04/Email-Statistics-Report-2010-2014-Executive-Summary2.pdf
2. www.slideshare.net/HubSpot/the-science-of-email-marketng
3. http://royal.pingdom.com/2011/01/19/email-spam-statistics
4. www.slideshare.net/HubSpot/the-science-of-email-marketng
5. www.forbes.com/forbesinsights/untethered_executive/index.html
6. www.marketingsherpa.com/article.php?ident=30037

Chapter 12

1. www.cio.com/article/660025/Taking_the_Risk_Out_of_Enterprise_Mobility
2. www.gartner.com/it/page.jsp?id=1278413
3. http://blog.nielsen.com/nielsenwire/online_mobile/consumers-and-mobile-apps-in-the-u-s-all-about-android-and-apple-ios
4. www.forbes.com/forbesinsights/untethered_executive/index.html
5. www.comscore.com/Press_Events/Press_Releases/2011/7/comScore_Reports_May_2011_U.S._Mobile_Subscriber_Market_Share
6. www.inmobi.com/press-releases/2011/09/28/inmobi-smartphone-study-reveals-41-of-mobile-users-to-buy-apple-iphone-5/
7. http://gigaom.com/2011/05/25/google-maps-hits-200-million-mobile-installs-as-mobile-rules
8. www.seomoz.org/blog/whats-the-future-of-mobile-search-and-seo
9. www.edisonresearch.com/home/archives/2011/05/the_social_habit_2011.php
10. www.bravenewcode.com/store/plugins/wptouch-pro
11. http://blog.nielsen.com/nielsenwire/online_mobile/consumers-and-mobile-apps-in-the-u-s-all-about-android-and-apple-ios
12. http://venturebeat.com/2011/04/28/almost-40-percent-of-app-store-game-downloads-were-free-titles-in-app-purchases
13. www.edisonresearch.com/home/archives/2011/05/the_social_habit_2011.php

Chapter 13

1. www.marketing.org/i4a/pages/Index.cfm?pageID=3322
2. http://dyn.com/dns-is-sexy
3. http://twitter.com/dyntini
4. https://foursquare.com/business

Chapter 14

1. www.youtube.com/watch?v=w4ooKojHMkA
2. http://zenhabits.net/the-reason-you%E2%80%99re-stuck

3. www.agilemarketingblog.com/wp-content/podcasts/MarketingAgility9-AlanBelniak.mp3
4. www.amrinternational.com/reports/b2b_online_marketing_in_the_united_states_assessment_and_forecast_to_2013

Chapter 15

1. www.prnewswire.com/news-releases/social-work-more-companies-permit-social-networking-on-the-job-robert-half-technology-survey-reveals-122650448.html

Index

ABtests.com, 149
ADG Creative, 132
Adobe Flash, 156–157
advertising options and services
    click-through rates and, 16, 26,
        143, 146, 149
    cost per engagement
        (CPE), 124
    Facebook ads, 59, 136–137,
        142, 151
    Facebook Sponsored Stories,
        136–137, 142
    LinkedIn ads, 59, 106–107
    testing, 142
    trending topics and, 124–125
    Twitter ads, 59, 124–125, 126
agile marketing, 181–182, 184
Alterian, 20
Amazon
    cookies and tracking
        methods, 162
    personal search histories and,
        37, 162
American Express, 125
Android smartphones, 156, 163,
    164, 166
annuity
    defined, 8
    social media as, 8–9, 96
Apple, 156
application programming
    interface (API), 50
apps, mobile, 163–165
App Used/App Shared
    Stories, 136
Argyle Social, 107, 115
"Art of the Sale" clip, 86
attribution
    defined, 47–48
    first- vs. last-action attribution,
        47–49, 52–53
audiences, building
    developing an audience, 9,
        21, xviii

targeted audiences, 56, 73
    See also reach, building
audio content, 85
author photos. See pictures and
    photos

Baer, Jay, 51
B2B (business-to-business) vs.
    B2C (business-to-consumer)
    marketing
    agile marketing, 181–182, 184
    direct mail vs. B2B social media
        marketing, 8–9
    marketing status quo
        and, 3–4
    reach building and targeting
        strategies, 55
    relationship-based sales, 5
    social media as tool for, 4–6,
        xviii–xix
    subject matter expertise, 5
    video content, usefulness
        of, 71
    See also social media
        marketing
B2B social media marketing. See
    social media marketing
B2BSuperStars.com, xxi
B2BWorkbook.com, xxi
Belniak, Alan, 181
Bing search engine, 32, 38
bitly, 36, 91, 111
BlackBerry devices
    blog and web views on,
        156, 160
    content creation for, 87
    mobile apps, lack of support
        for, 156, 163–164
Blendtec, 72
blog categories, 80–81
blogger.com, 82
blogs, content creation for
    company bloggers, recruiting
        and training, 81–82, 191

guest blog posts, 92
    mobile content, 87, 157,
        160, 164
    plagiarism, avoiding, 87–88
    video content for, 85–86, 87
    writing skills and, 74, 84–85,
        87–88, 96
blogs, lead generation and
    about, 77–78, 89–90, 93–95,
        118, 175
    as annuity, 8–9, 96
    audio content on, 85
    automatic publishing to social
        media and, 27
    business blogs, 79–92
    calls to action in, 89–90,
        96, 160
    corporate blogs, origins of,
        78–79
    engagement with readers and,
        90–91
    on Facebook, 91
    as hub of social media leads,
        77–78
    industry resource,
        becoming, 89
    interview experts, 96
    leads as trackable blogs,
        89–90
    leaving comments, 78, 91
    link building and traffic
        increases, 33, 35, 39
    on LinkedIn, 91
    Lynden Inc. example, 6
    measuring success, 91–92
    publishing/posting frequency
        for, 81–82, 88–89
    sharing content, 86, 91
    sharing e-mail content,
        87, 150
    on Twitter, 91, 118
    visual content for, 86
    white papers and, 79, 87
    WordPress for, 82, 160

blogs, setting up
addresses, 82
audio content, creating, 85
business blogging checklist,
84–92
content creation for, 17–19,
79–92
conversation, meaning in, 78
curated posts, 87–88
embedded polls in posts, 123
featuring blog content, 83–84
guest blog posts, 92
hosting, 82–83
mobile access to, 87, 130
nuts and bolts of, 82–84
optimizing content, 92
pictures and photos, 83
recruiting and training
employees to post, 81–82
thinking part of, 79–80
titles, 88
unified keyword action items
in, 36–37
Blog Tree, The, 86
Blumthal, Eric, 104
BMC Software, 85
Board Reader, 20
Boeing Airplanes, 123, xviii
Boggs, Eric, 107
BreakingPoint Systems, Inc.
blog categories, integration of,
80–81
blogs campaign success story,
44–46
brochures, eliminating, 88, 169
Brogan, Chris, 7
B-roll, 72
Burns, Lisa A., 72
business blogging checklist,
89–90
business blogs, 79–92
See also blogs, lead generation
and
Business Marketing
Association, 167
business objectives. See lead
generation process, social
media
buzz, generating, 63, 167, 170

calendars. See editorial calendars
calls to action (CTAs)
about, 14, 16–17
in blog posts, 89–90, 96, 160
click-through rates and, 16, 26,
143, 146, 149
in ebooks, 69
in e-mails, 143–144, 146
on landing pages, 26

publishing vs. marketing
perspective of, 16
testing and optimizing, 26
Careers tab, LinkedIn, 100
cascading style sheets (CSS),
157–158
change, resistance to, 190, 193
Check-in Story, 136
Chernov, Joe, 86
Ciena, 133–134
Cisco
B2B Facebook Pages and
Groups, 128
corporate blogging
initiatives, 78
video initiatives, 86
Citrix, 174
click-through rates, 16, 26, 143,
146, 149
cloud-based computing, 191
cloud-based video
presentations, 133
COCA (cost of customer
acquisition)
calculating, 42–43, 52
social media as good for,
46–47, 52
comarketing, trade shows as,
168, 175
company profiles. See blogs,
setting up; Facebook profiles;
LinkedIn company profiles;
Twitter B2B accounts
Comstock, Beth, 192–193
connections
asking for to build reach,
57, 140
e-mails for building, 149–150
LinkedIn requests for, 98
content
business value of, 17
vs. context, 16–17, 29–30, 161
content audits, 71
content consistency plans, 59, 62
content creation
audio content, 85
big ideas, sharing, 172, 180
for BlackBerry devices, 87
for blogs/business blogs, 17–19,
79–92
content discovery and, 19,
20, 27
for ebooks, 65–69
for e-mail marketing, 143,
145–151
entertaining value of, 66, 70,
72, 74
entertainment and interest as
goal of, 66, 70, 72, 74

for Facebook, 129, 131–139
LinkedIn company profiles,
97–100, 108
mobile content, 87, 157,
159–161, 164
mobile content creation,
159–161
mobile content for blogs, 87
people, talking about, 19
picking sides and opinions, 18
for reach building, 17–19,
58–59
remarkable content, importance
of, 17–19, 58–59
saying something new, 18–19
shipping and iteration,
frequency of, 22–23,
180, 184
speed of creation, rates of, 18
titles, 30, 67, 74, 88, 145, 151,
xviii
Twitter B2B accounts, 116–118
for video, 85–86, 87
video content, 85–86, 87
visual content for blogs, 86
for webinars, 69–71, 75
content discovery
consistent sharing and, 19–20
dedicated monitoring and,
20, 27
maximizing for lead generation,
17–21
reach building through sharing,
19–21
remarkable content, importance
of, 17–19
content discovery framework, 20
content offers. See offers
Content Rules (Handley), 71
content sharing
blog post sharing, 91, 118
blogs and, 91
e-mail and, 150
LinkedIn, business sharing on,
102–108
linking vs. social media sharing,
34–35
polls on Twitter, 123
on status updates, 102–103,
108, 133–135, 144
on Twitter, 91, 102–103,
117–118, 120–122, 126
Twitter chat, 122
contests
to drive site traffic, 175
on Facebook, 23–24, 137
reach building methods
and, 57
on Twitter, 120

context
  vs. content as king, 16–17
  as foundation of search, 29–30
  mobile content and, 161
conversion rates
  defined, 26
  landing pages and, 14–16, 26
  optimizing for lead generation,
    13–17, 26
cookies for tracking, 49, 162
Corning Incorporated, 72
corporate blogs, origins of, 78–79
  See also blogs, setting up
corporations, lack of public trust
    in, 78–79
Corson, Aaron, 106
cost of customer acquisition. See
    COCA
cost per engagement (CPE), 124
cost per lead
  estimating, 60–61, 125,
    126, 136
  reducing, 5, 75, 136, 137, 147
CoTweet Enterprise, 20, 115
count5, 104
CRM systems, 49–50, 53, 62, 101
crowdsourcing content, 170
CSS (cascading style sheets),
    157–158
cssZenGarden.com, 157
CTAs. See calls to action
customer relationship
    management (CRM) systems,
    49–50, 53, 62, 101
customers, understanding
  attribution and, 48–49, 52–53
  B2B vs. B2C marketing, 4–5
  information consumption
    patterns, 19–20, 79
  social media, lack of focus on,
    187–188

data analysis, as skill, 10–11,
    12, 41
data gathering
  Amazon tracking methods,
    37, 162
  business blogs, using for, 80
  customer relationship
    management (CRM) systems,
    49–50, 53, 62, 101
  Facebook Like button and, 35,
    58, 118–119, 133–134, 141
  Facebook News Feed and,
    129–130, 134, 141
  Google Reader, 88, 89, 106
  industry terms on Twitter, 122
  marketing and sales database
    integration and, 50–51, 53

storytelling using data, 196
  for tracking social media ROI,
    49–50
data storage. See CRM systems
"Day Made of Glass" viral
    video, 72
Dell, 129, 179
Digi-Key, 120
direct mail vs. B2B social media
    marketing, 8–9
"DNS Is Sexy" campaign, 171–172
domain name systems (DNS), 171
Domain Story, 136
Dyn, Inc., 171–172
Dyntini events and giveaways,
    171–172

ebooks
  calls to action in, 69
  content creation for, 65–69
  content links in, 68
  e-mail share buttons in, 87, 150
  emphasis boxes for, 68
  files names for, 68–69
  headers and headlines for, 68
  as infotainment, 66, 70
  pictures in, 68
  social sharing links in, 69
  takeaways in, 69
  templates and styles for, 67
  titles for, 67, 74
  Twitter, sharing on for lead
    generation, 120–121
  vs. white papers, 66, 68
Ecomagination Challenge, 36, 192
EdgeRank engagement
    algorithm, 130–131, 137,
    140, 141–142
Edison Research, 115, 160
editorial calendars
  blog publishing frequency
    and, 81
  content consistency plans and,
    59, 62
  idea shipping and iteration,
    22–23, 180, 184
  for LinkedIn information
    sharing, 102–103, 108
  monthly sprints, agile
    marketing, 181, 184
  for organization and time
    management, 188
  for regular content and reach
    building, 19, 20, 27
education websites (.edu
    domains), 32
Egeling, Mark, 105
80/20 rule, 37
Eloqua, 86

e-mail inboxes
  Gmail, 150
  Outlook e-mail, 150
  as pervasive communication
    tool, 149
  socializing, 150–151
  as social tool, 143
e-mail marketing
  benefits of, 150
  calls to action for in,
    143–144, 146
  clear expectations, need for in,
    149–150
  content creation for, 143,
    145–150, 151
  Facebook connections for,
    133–134, 149–150
  landing pages offers in, 146, 149
  lead generation with,
    145–148, 151
  LinkedIn opt-ins and sharing
    in, 144
  negative view of, 145
  publishing rates, frequency
    of, 144
  publishing/sending, frequency
    of, 148
  socializing e-mail inboxes for,
    150–151
  subject lines in, 145, 151
  testing ideas and designs for,
    143, 148–149, 151
  trust building in, 144
  usefulness in messages, need
    for in, 146
e-mail newsletters
  Facebook sign up for, 133–134
  opt-ins vs. calls to action
    for, 144
  Twitter, promotion of on, 119
e-mail share buttons, 87, 150
engagement
  bloggers and readers, 90–91
  EdgeRank algorithm, 130–131,
    137, 140, 141–142
  in e-mail marketing,
    measuring, 148
  Facebook and lead generation,
    138, 140–141
  Twitter, prospect engagement
    on, 123–124
exit strategies, 183–184
experiment retrospectives,
    24–25, 27

Facebook
  about, 127, 129
  advertising options on, 59,
    136–137, 142, 151

Facebook (*continued*)
benefits of, 127–130, 141–142
blog post sharing on, 91
content creation and sharing on, 129, 131–139
contests on, 23–24, 137
EdgeRank engagement algorithm, 130–131, 137, 140, 141–142
e-mail marketing and, 133–134, 144, 149–150
giveaways on, 137
lead generation and, 138, 140–141
lead generation on, 131–138, 140–142
mobile access to, 130
photos on, 135–137, 141
reach building with, 129
as search and discovery tool, 17, 38, 128–129
Sponsored Stories on, 136–137, 142
video platforms on, 137–138
Facebook Groups, 128
Facebook landing pages, 133–134, 141, 149
Facebook Like button
data gathering and, 35, 58
offers on landing pages and, 133–134, 141
Twitter, sharing content and, 118–119
Facebook Marketing: An Hour a Day (Smith), 127
Facebook News Feed, 129–130, 134–135, 141
Facebook Pages
advertising options and services on, 135–137, 142
Cisco company Pages example, 128
company website links to, 129
fans and lead generation on, 136–137
Liking a Facebook Page, 118–119
linking pages for leads, 132–133
vs. profiles, 127–128
websites, Page links on, 128–129, 175
welcome pages, 132–133, 141
Facebook profiles, 127–128
Facebook status updates
vs. LinkedIn updates, 102
posting content for lead generation, 133–135

Facebook Wall
posting content offers on, 134–135
posting newsletters on, 133–134
posting on others' Wall, 140
failure, accepting, 24
fans. *See* followers and fans
financial annuities, 8
first-action attribution, 48–49, 52–53
Fishkin, Rand, 158
Fitton, Laura, 110
Flash, 156–157
Fluke Corporation, 119
followers and fans
Facebook Like button and, 35, 58, 132–133
reach building, simplicity for fans and, 57–58
Twitter followers, gaining, 118, 125
volunteers, asking for, 123–124
Fournaise Marketing Group, 3
Foursquare, 164–165, 172–173
funding, social media project
B2B vs. B2C marketing, 5
benefits of long run results vs. paid services, 59
cost per lead and, 5, 60–61, 75, 125, 126, 137, 147
costs as roadblock to success, 188–189
overcoming cost and funding roadblocks, 188–189
start-up approach to, 182–183

Gartner, Inc., 155
General Electric (GE)
Ecomagination Challenge, 36, 192
GE Global Research, 83–84
giveaways
on Facebook, 137
at trade shows, 171, 172
See also contests; takeaways
"Global Marketing Effectiveness Program, 2011," 3
Gmail, 150
Godin, Seth, 180
Google
authority search and, 32
blog options on, 82
corporate blogging initiatives by, 78
current search algorithm used, 34
video site maps on, 73–74
Google+, 34–35, xx

Google AdWords
for e-mail marketing campaigns, 151
keyword research tool, 36, 80
vs. LinkedIn ads, 106–107
Google Alerts, 20
Google Analytics
blog hosting and, 83
for Facebook traffic, 131
for mobile traffic, 165
for monitoring and tracking, 20, 36, 50, 80, 131, 165
Google circles, xx
Google +1 feature, 35
Google Gmail, 150
Google Reader, 88, 89, 106
Google Webmaster Tools, 80
GoToWebinar, 69
groups
Facebook Groups, 128
Google circles, xx
LinkedIn Groups, 98, 103–105, 108, 175
guest blogs posts, 92

handheld.css, 158
Handley, Ann, 71, 116, 148
hashtags, Twitter
about, 114–115, 121–123, 171
#b2vchat hashtag, 122
#DNSIsSEXY hashtag, 102
#in business sharing hashtags, 102
headlines. *See* titles
HootSuite, 102, 109, 115, 122, 135, 188
Hoover's, 165
HTML5, 87, 157, 164
HTML vs. plain text, 147, 148
HubSpot
blog offers and calls to action, 89–90
as dedicated monitoring tool, 20, 50, 121–122
Facebook welcome page offers on, 132–133, 141
on lead generation and LinkedIn, 97
on lead generation and webpage content, 58
for unified keyword strategies, 36

ideas, generating, 22–23, 180, 184
inbound links
about, 32, 33–34
asking for from peers, 33–34
for reach building, 57
vs. social media shares, 34–35
trade shows and, 168

inbound marketing, 6, 39, 58, 116, 169
Indium Corporation, 82, 93, 179, xviii
infographics, 86
information (IT) departments, relationships with, 190–191
infotainment, 66, 70, 72, 74
innovation, failure and, 24–25, 27
integration
    blog categories and, 80–81
    in marketing and sales databases, 50–51, 53
    in social media marketing, importance of, 9–10, 11
Intel Corporation, 139
INXPO, 174
iOS operating system, 156
iPad tablets
    as contest prizes, 120
    mobile apps for, 164
    popularity of, 87, 157
iphone.css, 158
iPhones
    mobile apps for, 163
    mobile design and format for, 157–158
    popularity of, 156
    See also mobile devices
iterating, shipping ideas and, 22–23, 180, 184

Jobs, Steve, 24

Kerley, Christina "CK," 157, 165
keyword rank
    decline in, 37–38, 39
    rank, defined, 37
    vs. authority in search, 32–33
keywords
    action items and testing, 36–37, 39
    blog categories and, 80–81
    in blog posts, 80
    blogs, lead generation and, 36–37, 80–81
    context as foundation of search and, 29–30
    Google AdWords' keyword tool, 36
    in LinkedIn profiles, 98–99
    Twitter optimization on, 120
    unified keyword strategies, 35–37, 39, 80, 168
    See also search engine optimization
Khan, Irfan, 155
Kodak, 105

landing pages
    conversion rates of, 14–16, 26
    defined, 14
    "DNS Is Sexy" example, 171–172
    e-mail offers and, 146, 149
    Facebook offers on, 133–134, 141, 149
    "going naked" on, 15
    high-converting landing pages, 14–15
    mobile landing pages, 161–162
    testing and optimizing, 26
    tweeting, 119, 126
    vs. website pages, 14–15
last-action attribution, 48–49, 52–53
Launch (Stelzner), 174
lead generation process, social media
    basics steps of, 13–17
    blogs and, 77–78, 89–90, 93–95, 118
    content discovery, maximizing for, 17–21
    content discovery maximization and, 17–21
    conversion ubiquity, creating, 13–17
    e-mail marketing and, 146–148, 151
    on Facebook, 131–138, 140–141
    "going naked" in landing pages and, 15
    high-converting landing pages, 14–15
    landing pages and, 26
    leads, defined, 13–14
    on LinkedIn, 102–103, 105–106
    marketing testing frameworks, 23–25
    negative view of, 22
    offers and, 15–16, 22
    optimization and, 25–27
    as primary goal of social media marketing, 196, 197, xviii–xix
    reach building and, 17, 19–21
    shipping and iterating, 22–23
    test and fail fast testing methods for, 22–25
    trade *vs.* B2B publishing needs and, 16, 21–22
    on Twitter, 102, 109, 115–116, 118, 122, 135, 188

virtual conferences and, 173–175
    webinars for, 22, 69–71, 75, 121–122
leads, defined, 13–14
legal approvals, as roadblock, 185–186
Like button, Facebook. *See* Facebook Like button
link building success, strategies for
    about, 32–34
    blogs and, 33, 35, 39
    digital brochures for, 169
    inbound links into PR, 34
    linking to links in e-mail offers, 146
    reach building and, 57–58
LinkedIn
    about, 97
    advertising options and services on, 59, 106–107
    business sharing for value on, 102–103, 108
    content sharing on, 102–103, 108, 144
    customer acquisition on, 97
    e-mail marketing, connecting for, 149–150
    job listings on, 100–101
    networks, connecting and growing, 98–99
    Outlook and inbox socialization with, 150
    as search and discovery tool, 17, 38
    sharing blogs posts on, 91
    Twitter and, 102
LinkedIn Answers, 105–106
LinkedIn company profiles
    Careers tab, 100
    vs. company business cards, 99
    connection requests, 98
    keywords in, 98–99
    Products & Services tab, 101, 102
    profile pictures, 83, 99
    recommendations for, 101–102
    setting up, 97–100, 108
LinkedIn Groups
    about, 98, 103–105
    company-sponsored groups, 104
    connecting and networking with, 103–104
    for driving website traffic, 175
    joining and sharing on, 102–104, 108
    lead generation on, 102–105

LinkedIn News, 88, 102
LinkedIn status updates
    e-mail opt-ins sharing with, 144
    vs. Facebook updates, 102
    publishing/posting updates,
        frequency of, 102–103, 108
Livestream software, 138
location
    sales vs. marketing, 164–165
    trade shows and, 171–172
    virtual conferences and,
        173–175
location-based social networks,
    172–173
Lynden, Inc., 6

MailChimp, 134
management support, lack of,
    11–12, 46, 187
marketers, professional skills
    needed for
    accounting and budgeting,
        43, 52
    connection building, 57, 140
    data analysis and math, 10–11,
        12, 41
    failure, acceptance of, 24
    fearlessness, 46
    goal-oriented project
        management, 57, 94–95, 140
    leadership and management, 11
    overview of, 10–12
    storytelling, 10–11
    target audience, understanding
        of, 73
    writing skills, 74, 84–85,
        87–88, 96
marketing and sales database
    integration, 50–51, 53
MarketingProfs, 116, 148
marketing superstar lessons
    BreakingPoint Systems blogs
        success, 44–46
    Corning video market success,
        72–73
    GE Ecomagination Challenge
        success, 192–193
    Indium sales leads success,
        93–95
    Intel social media marketing
        success, 139–140
marketing teams, start-up
    approach to
    about, 177–184
    agile marketing and, 181–182,
        184
    big ideas, sharing, 172, 180
    executive support, lack of in,
        46, 187

exit strategies, 183–184
funding, 182–183
next-generation B2B team
    building, 10, 11–12
optimization, reviewing
    for, 182
passion for social media,
    building, 177–180, 184
shipping ideas and iterating,
    22–23, 180, 184
marketing tests. See testing,
    marketing methods
Material Safety Data Sheet
    (MSDS), 159
math and data analysis
    as marketer's skills, importance
        of, 10–11, 12, 41
    return of investment (ROI) and,
        42, 51–52
Mayer, Marissa, 157
meta description for optimization,
    31–32
    See also keywords; unified
        keyword strategies
Microsoft
    corporate blogging
        initiatives, 78
    Outlook e-mail software, 150
    on paid search and Yahoo!
        ads, 38
middle of the funnel (MOFU)
    offers, 65–66
mobile apps, 163–164
mobile content creation
    about, 159–161
    for blogs, 87, 157, 163
    company blogs and, 160
    context of content and, 161
mobile devices
    Android smartphones, 156,
        163, 164, 166
    BlackBerry devices, 87, 156,
        160, 163–164
    blog and website views on,
        156, 160
    iPad tablets, 87, 120, 157, 164
    iPhones, 156, 157–158, 163
    smartphones, 155–157
mobile marketing
    e-mail marketing and, 148
    Facebook livestreaming and,
        138
    location, sales vs. marketing
        and, 164–165
    popular content, discovering,
        165–166
    prioritizing mobile traffic,
        165–166
    site view testing, 166

websites, mobile-optimization
    for, 157–15
Mobile Revolution and B2B, The
    (Kerley), 157
mobile sites, 158
mobile style sheets, 157–158
mobile web
    Adobe Flash, 156–157
    iOS operating system and, 156
    landing pages for, 161–162
MOFU offers, 65–66
monitoring and tracking
    cookies for, 49, 162
    dedicated monitoring and
        content discovery, 20, 27
    Facebook News Feed, 129–130,
        134–135, 141
    online metrics, ease of tracking,
        10–11
    web analytics for, 20, 36, 50,
        80, 131, 165
monthly sprints, 181, 184
MSDS, 159

Nason, Josh, 171
NetLine, 87
NetQos, 44, 46
network administrators,
    relationships with, 190–191
News Feed, Facebook, 129–130,
    134–135, 141
newsletters. See e-mail newsletters
New York Times, 21–22
NJC Printing, 106
Now Revolution, The (Baer), 51

offers
    content offers, 74–75
    in e-mails, 146
    on Facebook landing pages,
        133, 141, 149
    Facebook Wall content offers,
        134–135
    lead generation process and,
        15–16
    location-based social networks
        and, 173
    MOFU and TOFU offers, 65–66
    sharing in social media,
        negative view of, 22
    social media content offers,
        74–75, xx–xxi
    titles of, 74
    on web pages, 14–16
    See also calls to action
Omniture, 20
online events. See virtual
    conferences; webinars
on-page SEO, 30–32

See also search engine
    optimization
OpenSiteExplorer.com, 39
optimization, 25–26
    See also search engine
        optimization
opting in, reach building and,
    57–58
Oracle, 163
Outlook e-mail software, 150

Page Like Story, 136–137
Page Post Like Story, 136, 137
Page Post Story, 137
passion, building, 177–180, 184
personal search histories, 37
pictures and photos
    on blogs, 83
    in ebooks, 68
    on Facebook, 135–137,
        141–142
    in Facebook contests, 137
    slides in webinars, 70
    in social media profiles, 83, 99
    tweeting, 123
    on Twitter profiles, 83
    visual storytelling, power of
        and, 135, 141–142
pivoting, 56
podcasts, 85
polarization in marketing, 11, 18
polls, tweeting, 123
Post-it Notes, 56
Products & Services tab,
    LinkedIn, 101, 102
profiles. *See* blogs, setting up;
    Facebook profiles; LinkedIn
    company profiles; Twitter
    B2B accounts
promoted account, Twitter,
    125, 126
promotions. *See* contests;
    giveaways; offers; takeaways
publishing industry/publishers
    thinking like, 16
    trade vs. B2B marketing needs,
        21–22
    web vs. print as medium, 22
publishing/posting frequencies
    on blogs, 81–82, 88–89
    of e-mails, 148
    idea shipping and iteration,
        22–23, 180, 184
    on LinkedIn, 102–103, 108
    reach building and, 58–59, 62
    on Twitter, 117–118, 126
    See also editorial calendars

Radian6, 20, 115

Radicati Group, 143
rank in search. *See* keyword rank
Rapportive, 150
reach, defined, 55
reach building, social media
    about, 55–56
    action, as essential to part
        of, 17
    better reach building questions,
        56, 61
    connections, asking for, 57
    content consistency plans,
        59, 62
    content creation for, 17–19,
        57–59
    content discovery
        framework, 20
    contests and, 57
    on Facebook, 129
    lead generation and, 17,
        19–21
    link building and, 57
    nearsightedness, avoiding, 61
    paying for reach, 59–61
    publishing/posting frequency
        and lead generation,
        58–59, 62
    sales/selling skills and, 56
    storytelling skills and, 58
    tangential reach, 56, 61
    targeting vs., 55–56
    through sharing, 19–21, 27
    time-tested methods for, 57–58,
        61–62
relationship-based sales, B2B vs.
    B2C, 4–5
remarkable content. *See* content
    creation
return on investment (ROI)
    attribution, first- vs. last-action,
        47–49
    calculating, 189
    COCA, calculating, 42–43, 52
    COCA, social media and,
        46–47, 52
    data gathering and, 49–50
    marketing and sales database
        integration and, 50–51, 53
    math of ROI, 42, 51–52
    measuring, 42, 47, 50–51
    sales cycles, knowing, 43
    social media, importance of
        in, 41
    social media ROI formula, 42,
        51–52
    TLV, social media and,
        46–47, 52
    TLV, understanding, 42,
        43–44, 52

trade shows and, 168
retweets, 113–114, 119, 121,
    146, 148
roadblocks to success. *See* social
    media roadblocks, clearing
ROI. *See* return on investment
RSS readers, 88, 106

sales
    existing tools, using, 71
    location, marketing vs. sales,
        164–165
    marketing and sales database
        integration, 50–51, 53
    reach building and selling
        ability, 56
    relationship-based sales, B2B vs.
        B2C, 4–5
Salesforce.com
    about, 38, 50, 51
    B2B mobile apps by, 163
    LinkedIn company profile for,
        100–101
Schmidt, Eric, 18, 155
Scoble, Robert, 78
search
    about, 29
    context as foundation of,
        29–30
    crowdsourcing content, 170
    first search engines, 29–30
    keyword rank and, 32–33
    keyword-stuffing and, 32, 34
    LinkedIn profiles and, 98–99
    social search vs. search
        engines, 38
    Twitter Search, 17, 20, 109,
        117, 122, 170
search engine industry
    competition to, 38
    current shift in, 38
search engine optimization
    (SEO)
    authority, changing, 32–35
    context as foundation of search
        and, 29–30
    key optimization aspects,
        30–32
    keyword rank, decline of,
        37–38, 39
    keyword rank vs. authority in,
        32–33
    meta description for, 31–32
    on-page SEO, 30–32
    page text and, 30–31
    page titles and, 30
    Twitter benefits of, 110
    unified keyword strategies and,
        35–36

search engine optimization (SEO)
(*continued*)
URL structure and, 30
video content and, 73
websites, mobile-optimization
for, 157–158
website traffic, driving and,
26–27
search engines
Bing, 32, 38
Facebook as, 17, 38
first search engines, 29–30
vs. social search, 38
Yahoo!, 38
YouTube as, 38, 73
See also Google
SEOmoz.org, 35, 36, 158
share buttons, 87, 150
shipping and iteration, idea,
22–23, 180, 184
Short, Rick, 115, 178
shorts meetings, 181–182
Siegler, M.G., 109
slides, webinar, 70
smartphones
about, 155–157
Android smartphones, 156,
163, 164, 166
BlackBerry devices, 87, 156,
160, 163–164
blog and website views on,
156, 160
content creation for, 87
HTML e-mails and, 148
iPhones, 156, 157–158, 163
mobile apps for, 163–164
See also mobile marketing
SMASH IT, 18–19
Smith, Mari, 127, 140
SMPs, 139
social advertising. *See* advertising
options and services
social media
about, 42, 51–52
as annuity, 8
passion for, building, 177–180,
184
as search and discovery tool,
17, 38
SEO, importance of to, 37–38
SocialMediaB2B.com, xviii, xxi
Social Media Examiner, 174, 175
social media marketing
B2B, when it isn't right for, 6–8
benefits and goals of, 3–4,
8–9, 41
changes in, resistance to, 190,
193
vs. direct mail campaigns, 8–9

executive support, lack of in,
46, 187
first movers in, 197
integration, importance of in, 9,
11–12, 50–51, 53, 80–81
lead generation as primary goal
of, 196, 197, xviii–xix
marketing status quo and, 3–4
polarization in, 11, 18
ROI, importance of in, 41
traditional marketing vs., 8–9
unified keyword strategy for,
35–36, 39
social media practitioners (SMPs),
139
social media roadblocks, clearing
change, resistance to, 190, 193
colleagues, lack of belief in
benefits, 193
cost and funding difficulties,
188–189
customer base, unawareness of
social media in, 187–188
executive support, lack of, 11,
46, 187
focusing and staying
objective, 94
global social media strategies,
scalability and, 192
identifying and predicting
roadblocks, 193
information technology (IT)
department, relationship
with, 190–191
legal approvals, 185–186
measuring tools and analysis,
lack of, 138–140
network access blocks, 186
skilled staff, lack of, 189–190
starting, lack of direction in,
191–192
steady innovative content,
maintaining, 73
time management and
organization, lack of, 188,
191–192
social media ROI formula, 42,
51–52
social network access blocks, as
roadblock, 186
social networks
Foursquare, 164–165, 172–173
Google+, 34–35, xx
location-based networks,
172–173
See also Facebook; LinkedIn;
Twitter
social networks, building and
growing

with e-mail connections,
149–150
on LinkedIn, 103–104
on mobile web, 151
See also specific social networks
social profiles. *See* blogs, setting
up; Facebook profiles;
LinkedIn company profiles;
Twitter B2B accounts
start-up marketing approach. *See*
marketing teams, start-up
approach to
status updates
Facebook, 102, 133–135
LinkedIn, 102–103, 108, 144
Twitter, 144
SteelMaster Buildings, 135
Stelzner, Michael A., 174–175
storytelling
importance of, 75
as marketer's skill, importance
of, 10–11, 12
reach building and, 58
using data and, 196
with video, 71–72
visual storytelling, power of,
135, 141–142
style sheets, 157–158
subject matter expertise, B2B vs.
B2C, 5
SugarCRM, 50, 51
Sun Microsystems, 78
superstardom B2B steps to
success
blogs, 96
content offers, 74–75
e-mail, 151
Facebook, 141–142
for lead generation, 27
LinkedIn, 108
mobile marketing, 165–166
reach building, 61–62
return on investment (ROI),
52–53
roadblocks, clearing, 193
search engine optimization, 39
start-up approach to social
media, 184–185
trade shows, 175–176
Twitter, 126
Sysomos, 111, 115, 123

takeaways
in ebooks, 69
for webinars, 70
tangential reach, 56, 61
targeted audiences, 56
targeting vs. reach building, 55–56
TBG Digital, 137

team building. *See* marketing
    teams, start-up approach to
TechCrunch, 109
testing, marketing methods
    e-mail marketing ideas,
        147–149, 151
    failure and innovation in,
        24–25, 27
    lead generation, test and fail
        fast testing for, 22–25
    marketing testing frameworks,
        23–25
Texas Instruments, 18–19
ThomasNet, 38
3M, 56
360 Signs, 33
titles
    for blogs, 88
    for ebooks, 67, 68, 74
    e-mail subject lines, 145, 151
    importance of, 74
    with keywords, 30, xviii
    SEO and page titles, 30
TLV (total lifetime value)
    social media as good for,
        46–47, 52
    understanding, 42, 43–44, 52
top of the funnel (TOFU) offers,
    65–66
TradePub.com, 87
trade shows
    big idea generation in, 172
    booths, inbound marketing
        approach to, 169
    as comarketing, 168
    "cooler" events for,
        creating, 172
    as coomarketing, 168, 175
    crowdsourcing content, 170
    following instead of collecting,
        169–170
    giveaways, using, 171, 172
    invitations, personalizing,
        169–170
    leads generation with social
        media in, 167–168, 169, 171
    locating-based social networks
        and, 172–173
    reaching building, online and
        offline, 173, 175
    socializing trade shows,
        169–170, 176
    Twitter, driving traffic using,
        171
    virtual conferences and,
        173–175
    word of mouth and, 170–172
trending topics, 124–125
Trust Agents (Brogan), 7

trust building
    corporations, blogs and lack of
        public trust in, 78–79
    in e-mail marketing, 144
    establishing in social media,
        169–171
TweetChat.com, 122
TweetDeck, 102, 109, 115, 117,
    122, 135, 188
tweets
    advertising options and,
        124–125
    landing pages, tweeting, 119,
        126
    mentions and replies in, 112
    photos, tweeting, 123
    polls, tweeting, 123
    retweets, 113–114, 119, 121,
        146, 148
Twitter
    advertising options on, 59,
        124–125, 126
    direct messages on, 114
    followers, gaining, 58,
        118–119, 125–126
    hashtags, 102, 114–115,
        121–123, 171
    lead generation tools for, 102,
        109, 115–116, 118, 122,
        135, 188
    LinkedIn and, 102
    off-platform benefits of, 110
    profile pictures, 83
    promoted accounts on, 125,
        126
    prospect engagement on,
        123–124
    publishing/posting tweets,
        frequency of, 117–118,
        126
    retweets, 113–114, 119, 121,
        146, 148
    testing ads on, 126
    trending topics on, 124–125
Twitter, lead generation and
    about, 118–122
    blog post sharing, 91, 118
    brand mentions, responding
        to, 122
    business sharing on, 102–103,
        117–118, 126
    contests, 120
    contests and, 120
    "DNS Is Sexy campaign"
        example, 171–172
    ebooks and white papers,
        120–121
    e-mail connecting with,
        149–150

    e-mail newsletter promotions,
        119
    GE Ecomagination Challenge
        example, 36, 192
    industry terms, listening for,
        122
    keywords, optimizing for, 120
    Liking a Facebook page,
        118–119
    linking to older content, 121
    methods for pushing the
        envelope, 124–125
    polls, sharing, 123
    reach building on, 17
    status updates, 144
    third-party articles, 119
    Twitter chats, 122
    video sharing, 119–120
    webinars on, 121–122
Twitter B2B accounts, 116–118
Twitter chats, 122
Twitterfeed, 27, 118, 126, 163
Twitter For Dummies (Fitton), 110
Twitter IDs, 112, 114, 116–117,
    121, 144
Twitter Search, 17, 20, 38, 109,
    117, 122, 170
Twitter status updates, 144
Twitter User Home Page, 111
Twtpoll, 123

unified keyword strategies
    blog content and, 36, 80, 168
    building, 35–36, 39
    testing keyword action items,
        36–37, 39
    trade show websites and, 168
URL shorteners, 58, 91, 111
URL structure, SEO and, 30

video content
    audio content, 85
    B2B video, three
        commandments of, 72
    for blogs, 85–86, 87
    B-roll, 72
    casting in, 72
    cloud-based video presentations,
        133
    content creation for, 85–86, 87
    on Facebook, 138
    humor in, 86
    length of, 72
    lighting and sound in, 86
    SEO and, 73
    storytelling with, 69–71, 71–72,
        135, 141–142
    Twitter, sharing on, 119–120
    viral videos, 72–73

video content (*continued*)
  web video *vs.* other formats,
    71–72
video site maps, 73–74
viral videos, 72–73
visual content. *See* infographics;
  pictures and photos; video
  content; YouTube
volunteers, asking for, 123–124

Walkley, T. Michael, 87
Wall Street Journal, 22
Walter, Ekaterina, 139
Washer, Tim, 86
web analytics
  blog hosting and, 83
  for keyword traffic driving
    review, 36–37, 39
  metrics, uselessness of some,
    197–198
  for mobile web traffic, 165
  for monitoring and tracking,
    20, 36, 50, 80, 131, 165
  for reach building, 62
  Twitter and analytics
    dashboard, 125
  for web and landing page traffic
    driving, 26–27
WebEx, 69, 174
webinars
  benefits of, 22, 69–71, 75
  content creation for, 69–71, 75
  e-mailing content to attendees
    for, 70

in-person audiences in, 70
  slides, using, 70
  takeaways for, 70
  on Twitter, 121–122
weblogs, 78. *See also* blogs,
  setting up
websites
  driving traffic to and analytics,
    26–27
  education websites (.edu
    domains), 32
  Facebook Page links on,
    128–129
  landing pages *vs.* website pages,
    14–15
  mobile-optimization for,
    157–158
  mobile sites, 158
  mobile sites, creating, 158
  mobile views of, 156, 160
  page text and keywords,
    30–31
website traffic, driving
  blog traffic, measuring,
    91–92
  link building and peer
    communication for,
    32–34, 39
  LinkedIn Groups for, 175
  optimization and, 26–27
  on Twitter, 121
  web analytics for, 26–27,
    36–37, 39, 165
web video. *See* video

web *vs.* print as medium, 22
white papers
  as blog content, 79, 87
  creating, 65, 66, 79
  vs. ebooks, 66, 68
  as LinkedIn content, 107
  sharing for lead generation,
    107, 120–121
  on Twitter, 120–121
WillItBlend.com, 72
word of mouth
  buzz, generating, 63, 167, 170
  location-based social networks
    and, 172–173
  trade shows and, 170–171
  on Twitter, 110
WordPress, 82, 160
WPtouch, 160
writing skills, 74, 84–85, 87–88,
  96

Yahoo! search engine, 38
Yelp, 38
YouTube
  about, 73
  "Art of the Sale" clip on, 86
  Facebook and visual
    storytelling with, 135,
    141–142
  as search engine, 38, 73
  viral videos on, 72–73

Zarrella, Dan, 143, 146

Get Step-By-Step Help from the Authors

Download The B2B Social Media Workbook Today!

Collaborate With Other B2B Superstars Today!

Join Our Exclusive Community!

It is time to show everyone in your company that you are a star. You can do it with the support of your B2B marketing peers.

Join *The B2B Superstars* at B2BSuperstars.com. This exclusive group of B2B marketers collaborates on strategies and works together to solve marketing problems. Led by Kipp Bodnar and Jeffrey L. Cohen, this group builds upon the strategies of *The B2B Social Media Book*, and provides education and support for implementing and executing B2B Social Media Strategies.

By Joining the B2B Superstars You Will:

- Collaborate with leading B2B marketers in an exclusive online group.
- Receive exclusive bonus chapters not included in *The B2B Social Media Book*.
- View exclusive, members-only webinars led by Kipp and Jeff on social media lead generation best practices and innovations.
- Ask questions specific to your B2B social media marketing challenges in live online video question and answer sections.

Don't settle for mediocrity. Leave the status quo behind.
Join *The B2B Superstars* today at B2BSuperstars.com!